HOW TO READ THE
LANDSCAPE

HOW TO READ THE
LANDSCAPE

A crash course in interpreting the great outdoors

Robert Yarham
Consultant Editor David Robinson

IVY PRESS

This edition published in North America
in 2018 by
Ivy Press
An imprint of The Quarto Group
The Old Brewery, 6 Blundell Street
London N7 9BH, United Kingdom
T (0)20 7700 6700 **F** (0)20 7700 8066
www.QuartoKnows.com

First published in the UK in 2010
© 2017 Quarto Publishing plc

Cover image: Alamy/Frymire Archive (bottom)

ISBN: 978-1-78240-602-0

This book was conceived, designed and produced by
Ivy Press
58 West Street, Brighton BN1 2RA, UK

CREATIVE DIRECTOR Peter Bridgewater
PUBLISHER Jason Hook
EDITORIAL DIRECTOR Caroline Earle
ART DIRECTOR Michael Whitehead
SENIOR EDITOR Lorraine Turner
EDITORIAL ASSISTANT Jamie Pumfrey
PUBLISHING CO-ORDINATOR Anna Stevens
DESIGN JC Lanaway
ILLUSTRATOR Coral Mura
PICTURE MANAGER Katie Greenwood

Printed in China

10 9 8 7 6 5 4 3 2 1

Contents

Foreword

Landscape comprises the visible physical attributes of our external environment. Some landscapes are heavily influenced by human activity, especially in towns and cities where they are often referred to as town or cityscapes. Other landscapes are much less influenced by the human imprint, and are more 'natural' although there are very few remaining areas that are true, pristine wilderness.

I was born and brought up in a rather grimy industrial city in the north of England. From an early age I loved to escape, on a bicycle or on foot, to enjoy the cleaner, more rural landscape of the surrounding countryside. This nurtured in me a love of nature and a desire to understand the landscapes I saw and visited. Although I now live in a cleaner, more attractive urban environment I, like many others, still love to escape into the country or to the coast, to walk, cycle and appreciate the beauty of the variety of landscapes that surround us, both here in Britain and overseas.

As an academic geographer, I am often asked to explain features of landscapes or the origin of particular landforms. Why is a valley, cliff or slope a particular shape? Why are we sometimes crossing bare rock, at other times on wet or dry soil-covered slopes, or crossing wet marsh or a bog? Why are some coasts characterised by impressive, vertical cliffs, others by cliff falls and slumps? Why are some beaches composed of coarse gravel whilst others are of fine sand or mud?

Many people share this curiosity about the environments they encounter and want to learn and understand more about their physical surroundings. Understanding the development of the varied landscapes they visit and the origin of specific landforms they see within those landscapes adds an extra level of richness to their experience of different places.

This beautifully illustrated book attempts to help people interpret the landscapes they encounter, in their everyday surroundings, on days out, or on holidays. For some, it may be a reminder of things they hazily remember learning at school or college, for others the information may be entirely new. What is undoubtedly different about this book is the way in which the contents are arranged as much as possible into 'landscapes', explaining how suites of features combine to give a particular and identifiable character to different physical environments. This is done through an abundance of carefully selected photographs and interpretive diagrams with a minimum of explanatory text. It is written by someone who shares through this book his love and understanding of landscapes, describes their characteristic features and explains their origin and evolution. The result is a valuable companion that will help many to obtain greater enjoyment and appreciation of places they visit.

DAVID ROBINSON, Sussex 2010

INTROD

For many people, there is little to match the unfathomable pleasure of a walk in an open landscape. The drama of the sea crashing against coastal cliffs, the silent majesty of the mountain tops, the vast emptiness of open plains, the desolate beauty of deserts, and the impressive power of grinding glaciers – all have their attractions. All of these sights reach to something inside us – perhaps a primeval instinct, a vestigial memory of the knowledge of the landscape that our ancient ancestors needed in order to survive. We still possess a sense of connection with the land. It is an ancient voice, programmed into our genes, that reminds us of who we are and where we come from.

The story of human beings is intimately connected with the story of the Earth beneath our feet, this small round ball of rock and water spinning in the empty blackness of space. Many of the minerals that each of us carries in our cells, in our bones, come from the substances deep in the ground that were forged when the Earth was just a glint in the eye of the Solar System. The great forces that gave rise to the shapes and forms of the landscape we see today also led to the development of all life on Earth, including us. The history of the landscape is our history too. And it is no wonder that thoughtful humans have often looked at that landscape and wondered how it came to be.

Fire and ice
Rock is subjected to many processes that form and shape it, from superheated depths beneath the crust to the grinding and shaping power of ice.

Looking for Clues

While the eminent 19th-century geologist Charles Lyell proposed his theory of uniformitarianism in his *Principles of Geology*, which was published between 1830 and 1833, it is sobering to remember that the Greek historian Herodotus, back in 450 BCE, found marine fossils in the Egyptian desert and correctly concluded that the rock layers had been laid down underwater many years before. The overwhelming urge to understand the landscape has obviously been with us for a long time.

Charles Lyell's concept of uniformitarianism, familiar though it seems to us now, proposed that the forces we see acting on the landscape today would have applied in the same way in the past, and therefore we can begin to draw conclusions about the gradual processes that shape the land, acting over unimaginably huge tracts of time. Applying what he had read in Lyell's *Principles*, a young naturalist called Charles Darwin, travelling on the HMS *Beagle*, found himself able to explain the long, ever-evolving history of the volcanic landscape of the Canary Islands, the mountains of Argentina, and the fossils that he found. Many years later, Darwin's discoveries would ultimately lead him to develop his theories of the evolution of all life on Earth.

Lost worlds
A fossil of an ammonite, an ancient sea creature locked in a rock, is a reminder of the many changes in climate and ecosystems that the landscape has witnessed over millions of years.

The concept of an ever-changing Earth is something that we have become all too aware of in recent years. Today we are beginning to understand how the climate and the Earth change and what their transformative effects may be on the landscapes that we inhabit. Throughout the Earth's history, the movement of the tectonic plates has meant that landmasses have shifted from warm, equatorial locations to harder climates over the course of millions of years.

Because of shifting plates and the changing climate, what is upland landscape today may once have been lowland desert. Softly undulating lowland hills may have been deep layers of sediment under the seabed. Green and lush hills and mountains may once have been at the heart of a volcanic region and later completely covered in thick masses of ice. All of the phases of rock-building, breakdown, erosion and deposition affect how the landscape looks today, creating the mountains, hills and valleys, and the rocks, silts, sands, gravel and soils.

Understanding where the landscape came from and how it came to be is what this book is about. It will help you look for and interpret the clues in every landscape.

Power of erosion
Rock exposed to the elements is subjected to powerful forces that break it down and reduce it to fragments – possibly none greater than running water.

Understanding the Landscape

Beneath every great landscape lies rock. In fact, beneath everything lies rock – of many different types, of many different ages and of many different forms, including rock that is not yet fully formed. Rock seems so static, so immutable that the phrase 'solid as a rock' is a universally

accepted truism. And yet these apparently unchanging building blocks of the landscape have been forged, shaped, destroyed and reformed over many millions of years, and are still constantly changing even today. The varied landscape around us is built on the foundations of change.

Understanding the Landscape

The landscape is characterised by its form and shape, by the vegetation and human habitation that cover it, and by the underlying rock and soil that you can sometimes see but that more often lies unseen beneath a concealing layer of plant life. Look carefully and it is possible to detect in these shapes the signs of how a landscape and its features were formed, sometimes by dramatic events over a short period, but more often by gradual processes over many thousands of years.

River power
The famous spectacle of the Grand Canyon in the USA was created by the erosive action of the Colorado River over a period of around 20 million years. During that time the water draining from the Rocky Mountains in the north cut through the Colorado Plateau to reveal many layers of sedimentary rock – shown by the lines in the exposed cliff faces – dating back 1,700 million years.

Ancient fault

While many valleys have been carved by the action of water or glaciers, the scale of some reveal a different origin. The Great Glen in Scotland nearly splits the country in two. It is thought to be evidence of an ancient fault boundary between continental plates some 450–500 million years old.

Great forces

The famous form of Uluru, or Ayers Rock, in Australia. The 500-million-year-old sandstone beds, of which the rock was formed, were tilted by movements in the Earth's crust (probably around 400 million years ago), and then gradually eroded by wind and running water.

Mountains of fire

Volcanoes such as Vesuvius fascinate geologists as they reveal so much about the Earth's unseen depths. They are formed by molten rock being forced up through cracks in the Earth's crust, which is why they usually occur near fault lines.

Ice peak

If the climate is cold enough, the build-up and motion of great blocks of ice in valleys gouge huge valleys and mountain peaks to leave characteristic shapes and features in the landscape, such as the pyramidal form of the Matterhorn in the Swiss Alps.

EARTH Introduction

Time's arrow
Geologists have pieced together the history of the Earth by charting and comparing layers of rock and fossil finds from all around the world, as well as by radioactive dating. The timeline below shows the different stages of the Earth's development.

The Earth coalesced from clouds of gases, ice and cosmic debris some 4,560 million years ago. Time on this scale is a difficult concept for the human mind to get to grips with, but it is crucial to being able to deduce when and how landscapes and their features were formed. In his book *The Restless Earth*, Nigel Calder famously compared the last 4,600 million years with 46 years in a person's life, only the last six years of which saw life emerge, with flowering plants appearing in the last year, dinosaurs passing away eight months ago, and all of human evolution taking place in the last hour. And during this time the landscapes we see today took shape.

History of the Earth's development

Aeon	Precambrian (Cryptozoic)							Phanerozoic			
	Pre-Archean	Archean			Proterozeroic						
Era		Early	Middle	Late	Palaeo	Meso	Neo	Palaeozoic			
								Lower			Upper
Period/ system								Cambrian	Ordovician	Silurian	Devonian
Epoch/ series											
Event	Formation of the Earth	First life emerges		First land-masses form	First multi-celled organisms			First sea creatures	First vertebrates	First land plants	First land animals
Date (mya)	4600	3800	3400	3000	2500	1600	1000	544	510	439	409

16 UNDERSTANDING THE LANDSCAPE

Meteor impact

The Meteor Crater in Arizona, USA – a fairly recent one created by an impact 50,000 years ago – is just one of many craters to be found on the planet that provide evidence of the Earth's bombardment by meteors since its birth, affecting its climate and geology.

Rocks of ages

Layer upon layer of rock tell the story of the planet and the many forms of life that have come and gone during different periods. Dating the layers, by comparing them with others, is complicated by the changes to the position of the rock wrought over time by geological forces.

		Mesozoic			Cenozoic							
Carbon-iferous	Permian	Triassic	Jurassic	Cretaceous	Palaeogene			Neogene		Quaternary		
					Tertiary							
					Palaeocene	Eocene	Oligocene	Miocene	Pliocene	Pleistocene	Holocene	
First amphibians and insects	Formation of first super-continent Pangaea	First dinosaurs and mammals	Break-up of Pangaea, first birds	Age of dinosaurs ends	First horses and primates	First mammoths	Formation of Himalayas	Formation of European Alps	First humans	First modern human	First civilisations	
363	290	245	208	146	65	58	37	24	5	2	10,000 ya	

The Earth's Structure

The Earth has a total circumference of 40,000km (24,900 miles) and a diameter of 12,732km (7,911 miles). At its heart is an inner core, essentially a ball of solid metal, mostly iron and nickel, around which is the outer core, comprising molten metals. Surrounding this is a thick layer, about 2,200km (1,370 miles) in depth, of dense silicate minerals that form the mantle. Floating on top of the mantle is the thin, hardened and brittle layer of the crust. The crust and the rigid part of the upper mantle, to which it is fused, form the lithosphere, the rocky base of the landscapes covering the planet's surface.

Blue dot
The Earth's cool, blue, water-dominated surface belies its fiery interior. The temperature of the inner core is thought be around 4,700°C (8,500°F). The heat rises through the outer core of liquid metal to the mantle, where temperatures can reach 3,500°C (6,330°F).

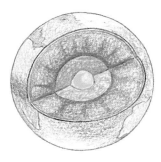

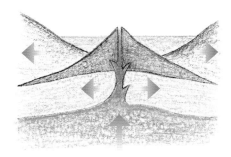

Driving forces

The heat generated in the Earth's core rises up through the rocks of the mantle, creating rising currents of heat. These currents cool as they move towards the top of the mantle and then fall back down again, driving the movement of the plates on the Earth's crust.

Ridge building

The discovery of the Mid-Atlantic Ridge, a volcanic mid-ocean ridge about 1,000km (620 miles) wide by 2,500km (1,550 miles) high where new oceanic crust is created, provided evidence to support the theory that the Earth's crust was continuously growing and moving.

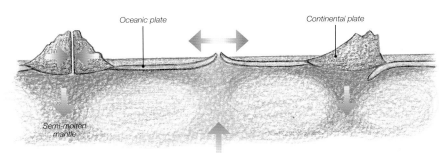

Oceanic plate

Continental plate

Semi-molten mantle

Going with the flow

Thanks to seismology and ocean exploration, we now know that rigid plates float on top of the semi-molten mantle (or asthenosphere), their movements being driven by the convection currents rising and falling in the mantle. There are two kinds of plate: continental plates (or sial, rich in the materials silica and aluminium), which are very deep and are made from older, lighter granite rocks, and the oceanic plates (sima, silica and magnesium), which are thin but are composed of very dense, younger basalt rocks.

The Moving Surface

Continental rift (right)

Iceland sits right on top of a constructive plate margin, a boundary between two oceanic plates. The heat and activity below the ground have raised the crust above the water level.

In 1912, the German meteorologist and geophysicist Alfred Wegener deduced from the shapes of today's continents, which appear to fit together like the pieces of a giant jigsaw puzzle, that they once formed a single 'supercontinent'. Post-war discoveries have since vindicated this theory, demonstrating that there are indeed plates that move about on the surface of the Earth. The movements of these plates, and the manner in which they grow and collide, cause the creation and destruction of mountains over enormous periods of time.

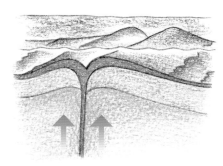

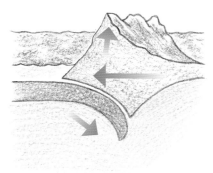

Constructive plate margin

The Mid-Atlantic Ridge is what is known as a constructive plate margin where two oceanic plates are gradually moving away from each other. As they do so, new molten rock (or magma) is driven up out of the ground, adding to the oceanic crust.

Destructive plate margin

This is seen where continental and oceanic plates meet. The oceanic crust, being denser, is forced underneath the continental crust. The continental crust buckles, creating mountains, while the oceanic crust descends into the mantle.

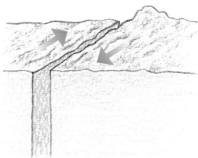

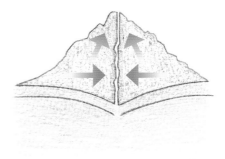

Conservative plate margin

Here two plates rub alongside one another, the friction causing vibrations, tremors and earthquakes. They are called conservative margins because there is no active creation or destruction of crustal rocks.

Collision plate margin

Where two continental plates collide, and one cannot slide underneath the other, they buckle, causing huge uplifts of rock. The Himalayas are created by the meeting of the Indo-Australian and Eurasian plates.

Introduction

As we have seen, far beneath the surface of the Earth heated rock stays in a semi-solid state because of the immense pressures being exerted on it underground. But every so often weaknesses in the rock open up as a result of plate movements on the Earth's crust. When this happens, the pressure on the rock reduces and it becomes molten magma, which is driven up through the cracks to emerge above ground in extrusions of lava.

Vulcanism
Volcanoes – such as the magnificent Mount Fuji in Japan – can be found all around the world in areas where plate movements have created stresses and weaknesses in the crust. In many places, the landscape features the remains of ancient volcanoes and deposits of volcanic rock.

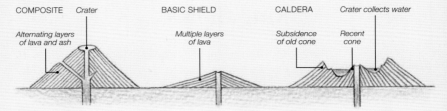

COMPOSITE — *Crater*

Alternating layers of lava and ash

BASIC SHIELD

Multiple layers of lava

CALDERA — *Crater collects water*

Subsidence of old cone

Recent cone

Cones of violence

Although there are many forms of volcano, the most obvious and spectacular is the classic 'composite cone' volcano. This is created by alternating forms of eruption – with layers of ash and then layers of lava being ejected and then deposited around the central magma vent over time. Sometimes volcanoes erupt with such force that they create large craters and carry lava and other fragmented materials into the air in huge pyroclastic clouds that rain down, spreading debris over a huge area.

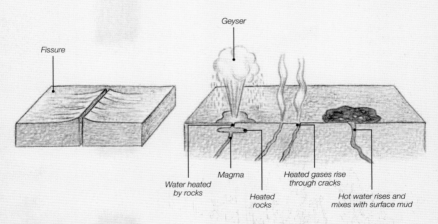

Fissure

Geyser

Water heated by rocks

Magma

Heated rocks

Heated gases rise through cracks

Hot water rises and mixes with surface mud

Fire down below

Volcanic eruptions don't always take the form of volcanoes. Where cracks in the crust open up as a result of plates moving apart, lava can find its way above the ground through fissures. Underground water can also be heated by magma, turning it to steam. The rising pressure forces the steam to explode up through the surface as a geyser. If the pressure drops gradually, steam can be released as a fumarole. Heated underground water can also mix with mud to create a mud volcano.

Making Rocks

Basalt towers
The extruded igneous basalt outcrop known as the Storr on the Isle of Skye was formed by layers of lava laid down nearly 60 million years ago, then eroded by the elements to create today's ragged shapes.

Crucial to the shape of the landscape is the type of underlying rock from which it is formed and how durable, or 'competent', it is in the face of the many erosive forces that it encounters. There are 30 or so rock-forming minerals that are commonly found on the surface of the Earth. These minerals, when combined in different quantities and under different levels of pressure and temperature, solidify to produce many kinds of rocks of varying properties. These rocks are grouped into three main types according to the process that formed them: igneous, sedimentary or metamorphic.

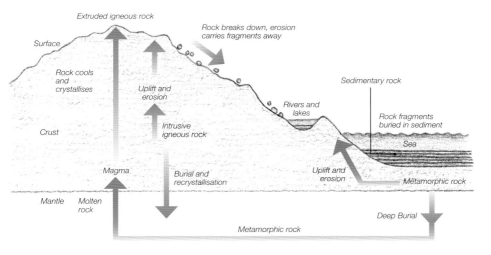

Extruded igneous rock

Surface

Rock breaks down, erosion
carries fragments away

Rock cools
and
crystallises

Uplift and
erosion

Sedimentary rock

Crust

Intrusive
igneous rock

Rivers and
lakes

Rock fragments
buried in sediment

Sea

Magma

Burial and
recrystallisation

Uplift and
erosion

Metamorphic rock

Mantle   Molten
rock

Deep Burial

Metamorphic rock

Rock cycle

Once molten rock has been forced above ground as lava, it is able to cool and harden over time, forming a rock called extrusive igneous rock. Magma can also form and cool underground, however, and the resultant rock is known as intrusive igneous rock. Both kinds of igneous rock are exposed and eroded over time, often being broken up and then transported by the forces of gravity, wind or water to a river, lake or ocean bed. As the layers of deposited sediments settle, the pressure

of other layers falling on top of them gradually converts them into sedimentary stone, such as sandstone or chalk. All rocks can then be raised by the buckling of the ground caused by plate movement, and exposed to weathering and erosion, which breaks up the rock particles and deposits it in sediments. Forces created by tectonic movement, the weight of sediment or pressures and heat deep underneath the ground cause rock to change, recrystallising in a new form called metamorphic rock.

Rock Deformation

Layer cake (right)
Folds in the vertical layers of rock demonstrate how the forces of tectonic movement can cause faults and bends in the rock strata to create mountainous landscapes like these in the Alps.

Once a rock has been formed, its journey has only just begun. The massive forces of plate tectonics can bend and distort layers of seemingly indestructible rock to lift up huge rock masses and create undulations and folds in the stone. As well as exposing rocks and sediments to the process of erosion through wind and water, such immense forces can compress rock to generate dynamic metamorphism, changing the rock's composition through intense pressure. This compression also causes rocks to crack and slip against each other, creating faults.

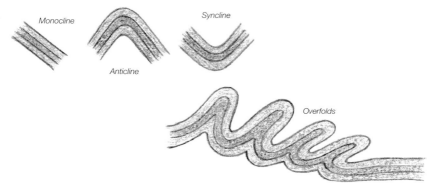

Monocline

Anticline

Syncline

Overfolds

Folds

All rocks, especially sedimentary rocks, can tilt, warp or fold when subjected to the huge pressures of the movement of the Earth's plates. Folds can range widely in size, shape and complexity, depending on the time and forces involved, from simple dips (monoclines), upward bends

(anticlines) and downward bends (synclines) to complicated multiple folds (overfolds). In all cases geologists rely on the law of superposition – new layers of rock sit on top of older ones – to deduce how and when the landscape was formed from the relative positions of the strata.

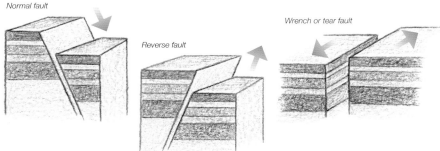

Normal fault

Reverse fault

Wrench or tear fault

Faults

When rocks are subjected to the stresses of compression, they can break and slide apart along planes called faults. The rock splits vertically, often at an angle, and one side slips down or is pushed up, so layers on one side of the fault are found much lower than their equivalents on the other side. Faults can also occur so that equivalent layers on both sides of the fault remain level with each other, as they are pushed sideways. Complex faults can occur at all levels in the rock, from the surface to a level that is deep underground.

Rock Breakdown

We have seen how rock is formed underground at high temperatures or under considerable pressure, but always in the absence of water and oxygen. Once rock is exposed above ground, it is at the mercy of the elements. Water in particular affects the chemical cohesion of rock, breaking it down into smaller particles of component minerals. In addition, physical attack by temperature changes and ice also weakens rock, making it susceptible to further chemical and physical breakdown. Over great periods of time, this wears down the rock and shapes the landscape.

Towers of strength
The mineral composition of the rocks and the forces acting on them determine how the rocks break down and are eroded, ultimately creating distinctive forms, such as the remarkable karst limestone landscape of Zhangjiajie National Park in China. Much of the rock has been dissolved away in the wet and humid climate to leave more durable pinnacles of stone.

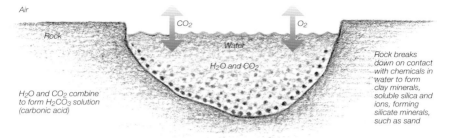

Air

Rock

CO_2

O_2

Water

H_2O and CO_2

H_2O and CO_2 combine to form H_2CO_3 solution (carbonic acid)

Rock breaks down on contact with chemicals in water to form clay minerals, soluble silica and ions, forming silicate minerals, such as sand

Chemical decomposition

Rocks are broken down chemically, or decomposed, when minerals in the rock come into contact with chemicals such as oxygen or carbon dioxide dissolved in water (also known as carbonic acid). These react with the minerals in the rock to create new minerals and smaller particles that can be washed away. For instance, rocks with high iron content rust as the oxygen from air and water reacts with the iron to form iron hydroxide. Small organisms, such as lichen, also secrete acids that can dissolve rock.

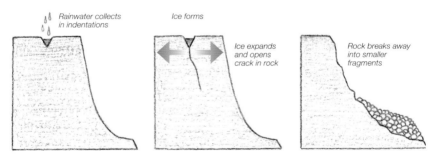

Rainwater collects in indentations

Ice forms

Ice expands and opens crack in rock

Rock breaks away into smaller fragments

Physical disintegration

The physical disintegration of rock – the breaking down of the rock into smaller particles – is caused by frost, extremes of temperature and organic attack. Water settles in holes and cracks, and then freezes, expanding and opening up the holes and loosening weak parts of the rock. Extremes of temperature – such as at high altitudes where rocks heated by the sun cool dramatically to subzero night-time temperatures – cause rock to crack and become more vulnerable to frost damage. Rocks are also broken apart by the roots of plants invading cracks. Burrowing animals, worms and ants can also expose the rock to damage by frost and water.

Erosion

After rocks have been broken down, the process of erosion carries the loose rock particles away and uses them rather like sandpaper to rub and scratch stone surfaces, opening up more weaknesses in the rock and exposing it to further breakdown. Gravity acts on the loose rock particles, as do the erosive agents water and ice, to pull them downhill. Wind can also pick up loose particles and use them to sculpt surfaces. All these forces strip down the rock to shape the landscape, gradually lowering it over time.

Wind power
The complex forms of these rocks demonstrate the power of wind erosion in deserts. Rocks shaped by the wind in this manner are called ventifacts.

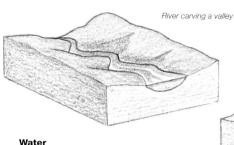

River carving a valley

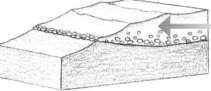

Glacier moving rocks and scouring a valley

Water

Water, already a key culprit in breaking down rocks, also plays an important part in erosion. Flowing water shapes rock and carries away small rock fragments and soil, and can even lift large boulders during floods. Waves also pound coastal shorelines.

Ice

Ice, in the form of glaciers, is another significant agent of erosion. It flows just like water, albeit very much more slowly. Glaciers pluck large boulders and stone fragments, which freeze into the ice, and then scour the landscape with the debris.

Wind carving a tor or pedestal rock

Harder rock

Action of wind

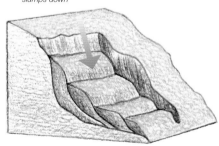

Unstable ground slumps down

Wind

Wind is much less dense than water or ice and so can only lift and carry very fine rock and dust particles. As with water and ice, the faster the movement, the larger the particles that can be lifted and transported.

Earth

Small rock particles and soil form a much less structurally stable mass than rock. Gravity, sometimes combined with water, causes these masses of earth and rock to move downhill in land- or mudslides.

Soil

A product of the processes of rock breakdown, erosion and deposition, soil is one of the most important substances on the planet next to water. Soil is composed of the particles of disintegrated and decomposed rock. It contains many minerals that were once part of the rocks they came from as well as decomposing organic matter, or humus, which has been broken down by micro-organisms and insects. Together, these materials support plant life, those creatures that feed on the plants, and ultimately a whole extended food chain of organisms, including humans.

Stuff of life
Green fields consisting of plants, grass and trees, and all forms of life that rely on them, are supported by the soil, the product of tiny rock fragments and organic material.

The good earth

Soil is a product of rock breakdown. In view of the moisture and acids it contains, including solutions of carbon dioxide and other acids emitted by plant roots and bacteria, it in turn further promotes the decay of rock. The types of vegetation supported by the soil depend on the composition of the original minerals released from the rock that form the soil, the organic matter decomposing in the humus, and the quantities of carbon dioxide and other chemicals. The diagram shows the development of soil from an initial, fairly barren substance – often found after the retreat of ice, for instance – to mature soil, after the decay of organic material and the work of micro-organisms, worms, insects and plants in the soil. Plant roots provide structure to bind the soil and sediments together, resisting soil erosion.

Immature Soil

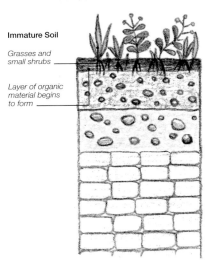

Grasses and small shrubs

Layer of organic material begins to form

Soil Formation

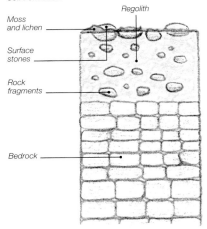

Moss and lichen

Regolith

Surface stones

Rock fragments

Bedrock

Mature Soil

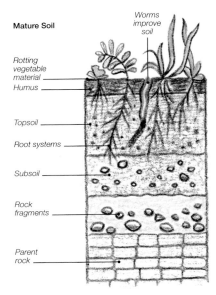

Worms improve soil

Rotting vegetable material

Humus

Topsoil

Root systems

Subsoil

Rock fragments

Parent rock

Deposition

Once rock has been broken down into smaller particles, the forces of erosion – mostly water, but also glaciers, wind and landslides – are able to transport the material to lower altitudes. When the rate of flow eventually slows, the particles settle, the biggest first, often in large deposits creating a layer of sediment. Over time more layers of sediment are laid down and, as explained on page 25, these layers are gradually transformed again into sedimentary rock. Then, one day, they are exposed and the process of breakdown, erosion and deposition begins all over again.

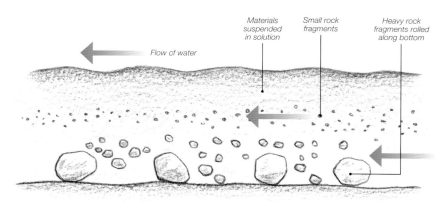

Materials suspended in solution

Small rock fragments

Heavy rock fragments rolled along bottom

Flow of water

Rivers, lakes and seas

Water is the primary force of deposition. Rivers carry huge quantities of sediment down mountainsides and hillsides. As the river slows, heavier rocks and pebbles drop to the river bed while the fine particles, such as sand or silt, are carried on down to a lake or to the sea. The particles are then deposited in fans as the river meets the sea. When rivers burst their banks, they create floodplains and deposit layers of sediment over the surrounding land. These deposits left by the rivers then provide fertile ground for agriculture.

Delta force

A river transports rock fragments that have been broken down upstream in the form of stones, gravel, sand, mud and silt. As the water flow slows when it reaches the sea in a delta, these particles settle, creating mounds of material at the mouth of the river.

Deserts

Desert dunes, also known as ergs, act as stores of vast amounts of sediment. In these very dry areas there are no rivers to transport the sediment, and so winds pick it up and sometimes carry it across the globe.

Glaciers

Glaciers pick up large quantities of rock fragments and carry them within the ice. After the glaciers thaw, large boulders and mounds of debris can be found lying in valley bottoms, left there by the ice.

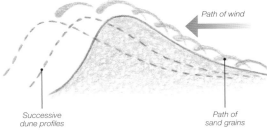

Path of wind

Successive dune profiles

Path of sand grains

Fossils

Lives past
The cliff face and beach at Lyme Regis in Dorset, constantly eroded away by the waves, reveal the layers of fossilised sea creatures that perished on the sea bed millions of years ago.

Fossils present a glimpse of how a landscape and the life that inhabited it were once so different. They can be found in sedimentary layers of rock that have been recently exposed by wind or water erosion, particularly in cliff faces. Such rock layers may once have formed the floors of rivers, lakes or oceans where the remains of underwater creatures, such as molluscs, were buried. Other fossils are found frozen in ice, preserved in airless and waterless conditions in a desert, or trapped in amber.

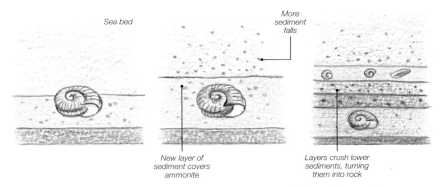

Sea bed

More sediment falls

New layer of sediment covers ammonite

Layers crush lower sediments, turning them into rock

Turned to stone

For an animal or plant, or its remains or traces, to be preserved in stone a rare chain of specific circumstances must take place. Perhaps the most common form of fossilisation is that which happens in sedimentary rock. The body of a sea creature, such as the ammonite above, drops to the sea bed where bacteria consume its soft tissue. Layers of sand quickly bury it and are slowly compacted so that they turn into rock. The minerals in the sediment gradually replace the molecules of the shell with their own molecules, thus preserving the shell. Eventually, the layers of rock are uplifted and then exposed by erosion to reveal the fossil.

Fuel for thought

Marine organisms can be buried to form limestone or crushed in sand to form sandstone. Fossil fuels are produced when plants are buried and, in certain conditions, they eventually form coal, oil and gas.

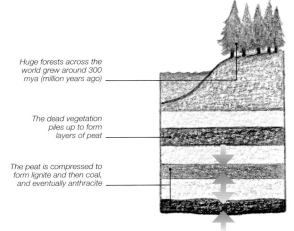

Huge forests across the world grew around 300 mya (million years ago)

The dead vegetation piles up to form layers of peat

The peat is compressed to form lignite and then coal, and eventually anthracite

Reading the Landscape

Part 1 presented just a glimpse of the many geological forces and factors involved in building, breaking down and shaping the landscape. This section sets out to show you how to interpret what you see according to where you are – in an upland, lowland, coastal or other type of landscape. Of course, no two landscapes are exactly alike, and each one has been subject to a complex history of geological activity. Part 2 describes just some of the processes that have shaped what you see. Note that processes listed under one landscape type, such as vulcanism, may also be found in other landscapes, but they have only been described once to avoid cumbersome repetition.

Amazon basin
Even vast, flat regions such as the Amazon have a long and complex geological history that has led to their current appearance.

PART TWO

Reading the Landscape

Shaping of the land
Uplift, erosion by rain, rivers and glaciers, and most recently human cultivation are just a few of the factors that have shaped the landscape we see here.

Determining whether the ground is mountainous, low, floodplain, coastline or desert, for instance, is a good place to start when reading the landscape around you. The next step to interpreting the forms in the land and working out how they were created and shaped requires some detective work. You can find clues to these origins by investigating the types of rocks left in the landscape, how they were raised or deposited into position, and how erosive forces or the shaping hand of human activity have affected them since.

Uplands

If the ground is high, then it has probably been raised in response to movements of the Earth's plates. However, as soon as rock is uplifted, the forces of erosion get to work and gradually wear it down.

Lowlands

Lower ground has been subject to tectonic movement, as well as subsidence and erosion by water, wind or ice. Lowlands often lie near to the sea and they are characterised by fertile floodplains.

Water and ice

Water and ice are responsible for the way many landforms look today, with running water and ice carving into and lowering mountains, creating river valleys, basins and floodplains, and shaping coastlines.

Human habitation

Of course, so much of the landscape has been altered by humans since we evolved into farmers. We've reshaped and farmed land, built our homes and powered our society using the landscape's resources.

Introduction

High places provide some of the most impressive and dramatic landscapes on the planet. However, while a mountain may seem the very embodiment of the immovable object, of serene and eternally motionless majesty, it is anything but that. Mountains exist because of the ever-changing nature of the Earth. They were formed, and are still being formed and shaped, by great forces acting over many millions of years.

Features of an upland landscape

A typical northern hemisphere upland landscape is subject to many forces during its lifetime. Plate movement lifts and cracks the underlying rock, and erosion wears it down, shaping the mountains, hills, rocks and valleys to create the features you see today. Mountains rise when the forces of uplift exceed those of erosion and mountains are reduced when the forces of erosion are dominant.

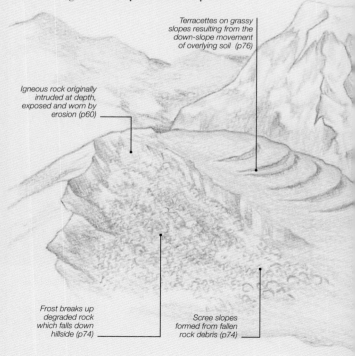

Terracettes on grassy slopes resulting from the down-slope movement of overlying soil (p76)

Igneous rock originally intruded at depth, exposed and worn by erosion (p60)

Frost breaks up degraded rock which falls down hillside (p74)

Scree slopes formed from fallen rock debris (p74)

The high country

Walk through an upland landscape and you encounter a wide range of different features: high peaks, often covered in snow in winter, rocky mountainsides, formidable outcrops of rock, cliff faces and loose stone slopes, steep-sided or wide valleys, waterfalls, mountain streams, lakes and tarns. Together they form a complex and varied landscape that owes its character to the underlying rock types and the forces of erosion (water, wind and ice) and deposition that have acted on it.

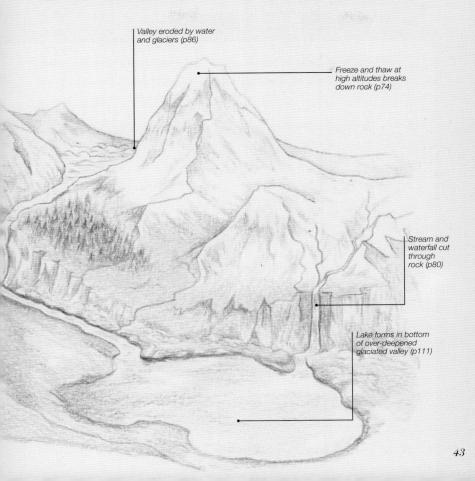

Valley eroded by water and glaciers (p86)

Freeze and thaw at high altitudes breaks down rock (p74)

Stream and waterfall cut through rock (p80)

Lake forms in bottom of over-deepened glaciated valley (p111)

Mountain Ranges

Roof of the world
The impressive Himalayas were created when the Asian and Indian continental plates collided 70 mya. They are still rising at a rate of 5mm (¼ in) each year.

Mountain ranges come in all shapes and sizes. Some are very old – sometimes more than 400 million years old – whereas others, comparatively speaking, are much younger. By and large, the higher the mountain range you're travelling through, the younger it is. Of course, most mountains are the way they are as the result of a long and complex series of geological events, and ranges often include mountains formed from a variety of rock types, of different degrees of hardness and competence (stiffness).

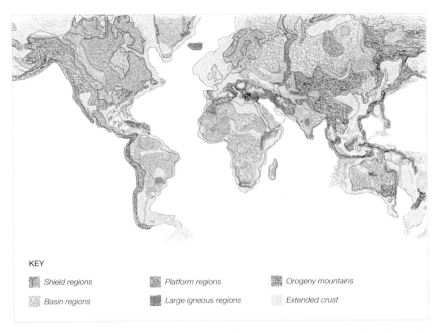

KEY

🟦 Shield regions   🟦 Platform regions   🟦 Orogeny mountains

🟦 Basin regions   🟦 Large igneous regions   🟦 Extended crust

Mountain ranges of the world

Most mountains have been created in a process of uplift, known as orogenesis, when forces of horizontal compression fold and raise the layers of rock laid down by millions of years of deposition. The tectonic forces also cause cracks, or faults, to open up, forcing the ground to split and rise or fall. Mountains are also formed by molten rock being pushed up to or near the surface of the ground; this tends to happen around areas of extreme tectonic activity, where plates are colliding or being pulled apart.

These mountain ranges have been formed and shaped during extremely prolonged periods of activity. For instance, the Caledonian massif, which stretches across Norway and Scotland, was created around 400 mya. It was lifted up when plates collided into each other. Later tectonic forces inspired periods of igneous and volcanic activity in Britain, the signs of which can still be found in the rocks along the western side of the country. Since then, erosion has gradually worn away much of the exposed rock.

Forming a Mountain Range

Sometimes you may come across exposed layers of sedimentary rock in the landscape that show large 'bends' in what were once straight, flat layers of rock. These folds in the rock have been caused over considerable time by the immense forces of compression generated by the Earth's plates pushing against one another. The same principle applies on a much larger scale to how many mountains were formed.

Rock folds

Occasionally, folded layers of rock are exposed by erosion. These indicate how rock can be bent to create undulating landscapes typical of uplands. Subsequent cracks or faults in the ground, also caused by pressures of plate movement, can complicate the pattern of rock still further to create areas of differing hardness and resistance to erosion.

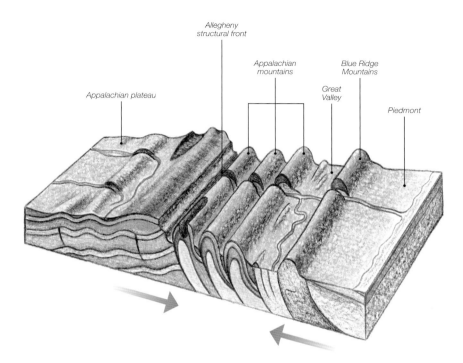

Allegheny
structural front

Appalachian
mountains

Blue Ridge
Mountains

Great
Valley

Appalachian plateau

Piedmont

Origin of mountains

The process of mountain folding can be compared to what happens to a cloth on a smooth table when you push the material together from opposing sides. When compressed by tectonic forces, layers of rock, represented by the cloth, rise up in folds and corresponding dips or valleys. The compression also creates multiple underground, angled faults, which push the layers of rock out of alignment. The Appalachian mountains (a series of mountain ranges that extend for around 2,400km/1,500 miles across the northeastern USA) are a good example of this form of mountain building. It is thought that they began forming around 470 mya as a result of the collision between plates that created the supercontinent known as Pangaea (a term coined by 19th-century German scientist Alfred Wegener). Subsequently, a combination of further plate collisions and erosion continued to shape the Appalachians.

Flat-topped Mountains

Great Rift

The Great Rift Valley in East Africa is part of a complex of faults that are constantly opening as the smaller Somalian plate pulls apart from the Nubian plate that forms most of Africa.

Large flat-topped mountains or plateaux with wide, steep-sided valleys have often been formed by extensive parallel cracking of the ground. The stretching (or compression) of a plate can cause multiple faults to open up along one axis, creating several aligned features. As well as raising and tilting blocks to create fault block mountains, the ground may also subside, sliding down to create corresponding rift valleys. An example of this sort of landscape can be found in the Great Rift Valley in East Africa and the Rhine Valley in Germany.

Cracked open

Continued stresses in the ground deepen and widen the parallel cracks still further. The blocks of rock begin to slip past each other to create wide, shallow valleys.

Pulled apart

Pulled apart

As the crust is gradually pulled apart by tectonic forces, tension in the underlying rock creates huge vertical cracks that form at different angles down into the ground.

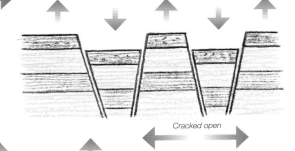

Cracked open

Slip and slide

As some blocks of ground slowly slip further down, others rise up, creating large, mountainous areas separated by lines of deep valleys.

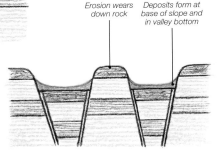

Erosion wears down rock   *Deposits form at base of slope and in valley bottom*

Erosion

Erosion wears away the tops and edges of the cliffs to create slopes of debris along the sides of the valleys. Running water deposits the debris as sediment in valley lakes.

Steep Mountainsides

Raised mountains

The Teton mountain range in Wyoming forms part of the Rocky Mountains. The steep eastern scarp rises to over 2,100m (6,890ft) above its base in the valley called Jackson Hole.

A line of steep-sided mountains beside a flat valley floor can indicate that the mountains were raised up when long cracks opened in the ground as the crust was pulled apart and thinned by tectonic forces. Mountain ranges formed in this way often have one very steep escarpment on one side, where the two blocks cracked and slid apart, and a gentle slope on the other side, leading down from the summit. The Grand Tetons in the USA are a good example of this, as is, on a smaller scale, the scarp of Cross Fell that rises above the Vale of Eden in Cumbria in the UK.

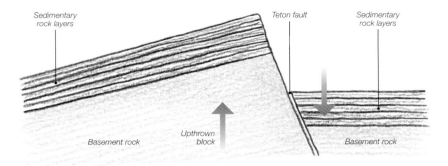

Uplifted mountains

The Grand Tetons in Wyoming were formed between 600 and 900 mya by the splitting of the ground along a huge crack, or fault. The rock on one side of the fault was forced up and the neighbouring ground slipped down, creating a huge cliff rising up between them. The evidence for this split is found in the differing heights of what remains of the original rock layers on either side of the fault.

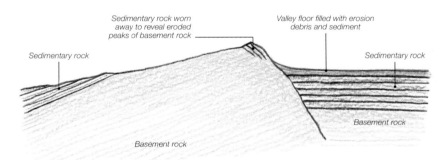

Eroded peaks and valleys

Over time, erosion has gradually worn away the exposed upper layers of soft sedimentary rock on top of the uplifted mountains, exposing the basement rock and creating the jagged and uneven points of the Teton peaks themselves. Water has gradually washed away the debris resulting from the breakdown and erosion of the rocks and deposited it in new layers of sediment on the flat valley floor.

Erosive Forces

Aira Force

Aira Force waterfall in the English Lake District displays the erosive power of water, which carries sediment and fragments of rock that abrade the rock below.

Over the preceding pages we have been finding out how mountain ranges were formed when huge areas of ground and rock were pushed, lifted, folded and cracked by tectonic activity. But this is only half the story: erosion is just as much of a factor in shaping the landscape we see today. Water, frost, wind, gravity and glaciers can exploit the weaknesses in exposed rock as a result of its composition, and create and widen the cracks.

Earth movement and rock falls

Rock weakened by weathering and erosion crumbles and falls down mountains and hillsides. Under the influence of water and gravity, soil can also slip and flow or slide to shape the upland landscape.

Running water

The primary agent of erosion is water, and as it flows down the mountains and hills, forming streams, rivers, rapids and waterfalls, it cuts through the rock and soil, creating new and spectacular landforms.

Frost and ice

We saw in Part 1 how frost and ice at high altitudes damage rock. They are key factors in causing mountain tops to break up and erode. Gravity, melting ice and water then carry the fragments downhill.

Ice and glaciers

Glaciers develop during prolonged periods of cold weather and precipitation (as snow). Several ice ages in the last two million years brought glaciers that shaped large areas of uplands in the northern hemisphere.

Rocky Peaks

Upland landscapes are peppered with rocky outcrops and summits. Naturally, ice and water erosion have played a large part in creating these uneven and jagged landscapes. Whereas some softer and weaker rocks crack and break down easily, others tend to be more durable. These harder rocks, usually consisting of igneous rocks, such as granite, take longer to erode and decay and so stand higher for longer. Many prominent peaks in Britain, such as in the Lake District or Scottish Highlands, consist of these igneous rocks that were uplifted and then exposed.

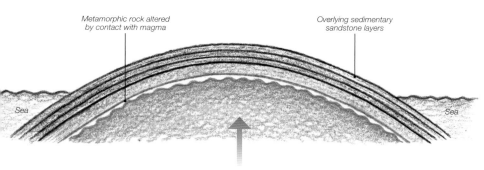

Metamorphic rock altered by contact with magma

Overlying sedimentary sandstone layers

Sea

Sea

Rising molten magma

Uplifting experience

The combined processes of uplift and erosion of igneous rocks are responsible for creating many peaks, such as those that crown the Isle of Arran, off the west coast of Scotland. Around 60 mya, during the Tertiary period, magma from far below the Earth's surface was forced up in a huge, underground dome-shaped mass. As it rose, the magma lifted and bent the overlying layers of sedimentary rocks. This upward bulge now forms the island of Arran.

The peaks of Arran

The hard granite peaks of Goat Fell, on Arran, are the exposed remains of a huge domed mass of magma from deep below the ground. Millions of years of rock breakdown and erosion have created the jagged outcrops we see today. Peaks like these often show signs of glacial erosion as well (see page 102).

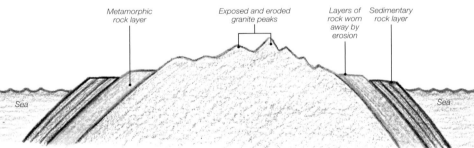

Metamorphic rock layer

Exposed and eroded granite peaks

Layers of rock worn away by erosion

Sedimentary rock layer

Sea

Sea

Granite rock

Peak erosion

The magma then solidified to form granite rock. Magma that hardens slowly underground forms large crystals, such as those found in granite, making the rock much more resistant to breakdown and erosion. Gradually, the upper, soft layers of sedimentary rock have been worn away by the action of frost, running water and ice to expose the harder granite rock lying beneath, which has then also been eroded and shaped by the same agents.

Isolated Rock Masses

In upland areas, particularly in arid regions, some rock masses, peaks or smaller rocks may stand alone or isolated in the landscape, instead of forming part of a larger, continuous range. These outcrops are often what remains of large blocks of sedimentary rocks after the processes of erosion by streams (or glaciers in what were once cold regions), rock breakdown and rock falls have taken effect. The remaining outcrops are known as mesas, which are eventually reduced to smaller pinnacles, or buttes.

Monument mesas
These mesas and buttes in Monument Valley, on the Arizona/Utah border, USA, represent all that is left of what was once a continuous mass of rock. The layers of sediment have been broken down by frost action and rock falls, and eroded by the flow of desert streams.

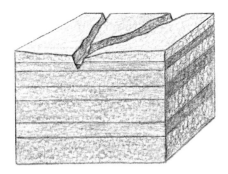

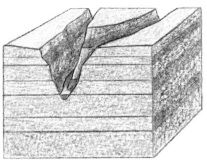

Sediments laid down

Layers of sediment are gradually deposited by rivers in large estuaries, lakes or oceans. These sediments harden to form large, flat layers of rock, which become subject to breakdown and erosion by running water the moment they are exposed.

Erosion

Stream systems develop that cut valleys into the rock, gradually carrying away stone fragments. Rock breakdown is precipitated by attack by frost, and rock falls carry the rock fragments down the cliff into the valleys below.

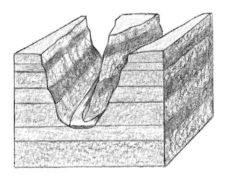

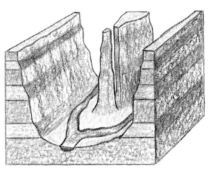

Retreat

Because there is very little precipitation in arid regions, the tops of the rock remain little affected by erosion. Instead, the near-vertical rock walls slowly retreat as they continue to break down and fall away, eroded by the streams at their feet.

Islands of rock

Some islands and smaller towers of rock, known as mesas and buttes, remain but these rock forms will also eventually be worn down by weathering and rock falls like the surrounding landscape, the fragments being carried away by streams.

Large, Angled Ridges

Rundle strip
Mount Rundle in Alberta, Canada owes its distinctive 'hog-back' form to the way that its layers of rock have been bent upwards and then worn away by many years of erosion.

Some tall ridges have a steep slope on one side, known as an escarpment, and a more gentle slope on the other – similar to some mountainsides (page 50). These ridges have been created by different processes, however. Again, plate tectonics have played a role, by distorting the underlying layers of rock, but erosion has then cut away layer upon layer of exposed, softer rock to create the dramatic ridge we see today.

Folding

Flat layers of sedimentary rock are gradually pushed up by compression resulting from plate movement, raising them up into great undulating folds.

Rainwater and ice exploit cracks

Erosion

Erosion immediately begins to wear away the layers of rock, flowing water exploiting vertical stress fractures that formed in the rock through the layers as they were bent.

Water

The weaknesses in the rock are gradually exposed and the rock breaks down, water washing away the debris and cutting down further into the layers.

Rivers cut valleys

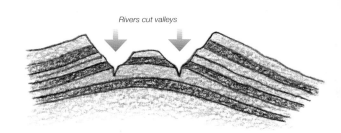

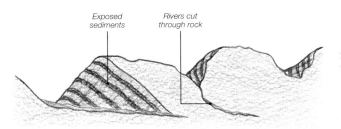

Exposed sediments

Rivers cut through rock

Ridge takes shape

Running water may also flow across the ridge, cutting V-shaped valleys through what is known as a hog-back, to create a distinctive 'flat-iron' shape.

Large Flat-topped Rocks

Table top
Mount Garajonay
on the island of
La Gomera in the
Canary Islands is
formed of an area
of volcanic rock
that has resisted
the erosion that
has worn away
the surrounding
landscape features.

Large, flat-topped rocks have been created by a prolonged
process of erosion that has worn away the surrounding
material, leaving behind harder islands of rock standing
tall. Also called mesas (see page 56), these features are
often associated with arid areas. The flat tops of these
rocks often comprise a cap of durable rock, usually
consisting of harder better-cemented sediments, that
protects the softer layers beneath. Smaller pinnacles of
rock, known as buttes, are formed in the same way.

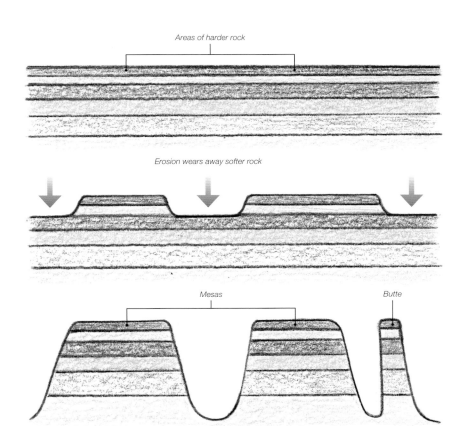

Areas of harder rock

Erosion wears away softer rock

Mesas *Butte*

Formation of flat-topped rocks

Successive layers of sediment that have been laid down over many years of deposition collect on top of each other. Some areas of the rock are harder and more competent than others because of various factors influencing their creation, such as component minerals, chemical reactions or greater pressures present when the rock formed. The exposed layers of rock are eroded by water or wind, which cut down into the layers where the rock is softest. This lowers the ground except where the surface is protected by hard caps of rock. Gradually, table-like rock formations emerge. These may be angled, if the layers of sediment were folded during their history.

Active Volcanoes

Eerie Etna
The sides of the dark and brooding Mount Etna, on the island of Sicily in the Mediterranean, are formed from layers of ash and lava that have been spewed out from its vents. Etna is the highest active volcano in Europe.

An active volcanic landscape seems at once alien and disturbing, probably because of the glimpse it provides of the tremendous forces at work beneath our feet, shaping our planet. Most active volcanoes lie near active plate boundaries. Characterised by rising cones or domes of volcanic material, mountain-top craters and flows of lava and ash, the shape of an active volcano depends on how it has been formed and what material it is made from. Some volcanoes, such as Mount St Helens in Washington State, USA, can erupt explosively.

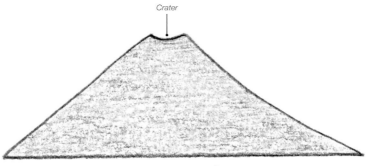

Crater

Composite volcano

These are large, steep-sided, symmetrical volcanoes, such as Mount Etna or Mount Fuji in Japan. Their sides are built up by alternating layers of lava, ash and rock fragments ejected by eruptions.

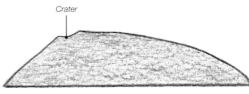

Crater

Cinder cone

A cinder cone is created when plumes of ash, cinders and other coarse fragments are ejected, building up a mound around the vent. Lava may also flow from vents around the base of the cone.

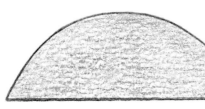

Lava dome

When the lava is very dense, and there is very little gaseous content, it hardly flows at all and instead solidifies very quickly over the vent in dome-like forms. Over time, these flows build up lava domes or plugs.

Crater or caldera

Shield volcano

These are broad, convex domes formed by eruptions of hot, free-flowing lava that covers a large surface area. Shield volcanoes, such as Mauna Loa in Hawaii, USA, can cover hundreds of square kilometres/miles.

Craters

Some regions still show visible and obvious signs of past volcanic activity in the form of a chain of mountains or hills, some of which may still have craters at their summits. These mounds and craters have been created by the eruption of material through holes in the ground and subsequently, in the absence of frequent volcanic activity, have broken up and been eroded. As they are relatively recent features, at least geologically speaking, erosion has not had enough time to wear them down completely.

Spent forces
The Chaîne des Puys in the Massif Central in France is what remains of a line of extinct volcanoes, in the form of cinder cones, lava domes and maars (large craters formed by explosions of groundwater when it comes into contact with the molten magma). They were last active about 6,000 years ago.

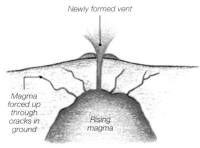

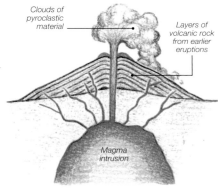

Rising magma

Magma pushes up to the surface, creating a bulge in the ground. Cracks form, allowing the magma to force its way up to the surface either through a central vent or through multiple side vents.

Eruption

During their active life, eruptions spew a range of materials around the vent, including water, gases, molten lava, ash and fragments of rock. These build up the sides of the volcano into a mound.

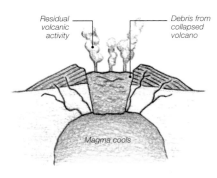

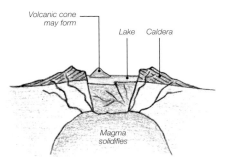

Reduced activity

As the volcano becomes less active, erosion wears away the dome and central vent of the volcano, widening the crater. The edges of the crater subside to create a larger crater or caldera.

Decay and erosion

Gradually, long-term erosion widens the caldera still further, and it often fills up with water. Continued volcanic activity may result in smaller, newer cones appearing inside the caldera.

Rock Towers

The columns of magma that once stretched up through the ground to form the cores or 'necks' of volcanoes often leave behind harder rock than the surrounding sedimentary or metamorphic rock through which they forced their way millions of years ago. As we have seen, once the elements begin to wear down the rock in a landscape, the hardened magma is often the last to disappear, and so it results in much more durable features.

Devils Tower
This tower of igneous rock in Wyoming, in the USA, stands above the surrounding sedimentary rock. Geologists are still discussing its exact origins, but one current theory is that the tower is composed of magma that formed inside the base of a large volcano.

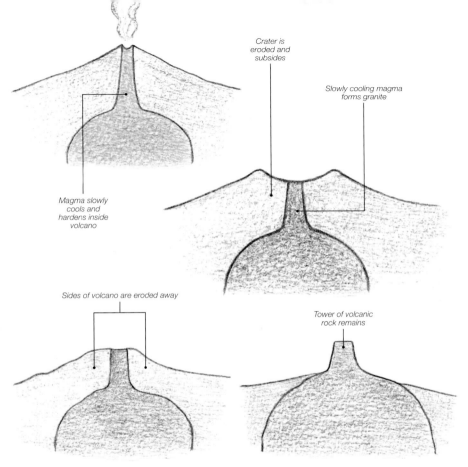

Magma slowly cools and hardens inside volcano

Crater is eroded and subsides

Slowly cooling magma forms granite

Sides of volcano are eroded away

Tower of volcanic rock remains

Formation of a volcanic tower

Once a volcano has become extinct, the columns or chambers of magma that fed it solidify slowly underground, forming harder material than the surrounding sedimentary or metamorphic rock. As the volcanic ash and other rock in the landscape are eroded and washed away by the action of rainfall and glaciers, the harder volcanic rock remains, forming an outcrop that stands out vertically in the landscape. This is further eroded by rain, ice and frost, and shaped by glaciers to create the rocky tower that we see today.

Lava

Volcanic eruptions result in different types of lava flow. These are easy to identify when fresh, but many become eroded over time, often leaving remnants of dark igneous rock behind. The most easily identifiable type of ancient lava is the basalt columns found in different parts of the world, although you may also encounter large areas of dark, fine-grained rock created by lava flows, dykes or intrusions into surrounding rock or, rarely, the rounded pillow lava that was formed underwater.

Lava colums

Columns of basalt rock formed as the lava cooled very slowly, causing evenly spaced fissures to appear. These rock formations are often revealed on exposed cliffs or coastlines, such as on the Giant's Causeway in Northern Ireland, or on the island of Staffa in Scotland.

Fresh lava flow

Basaltic lavas are fluid and flows come in two characteristic forms: pahoehoe lava with a smooth or ropey surface and a'a lava, which is rougher and lumpier in appearance. Andesitic lava is more viscous and produces lava with a blocky texture.

Consolidated lava

Some lavas flow across or are forced through older rocks and become consolidated with them, resulting in lava forms that appear, when exposed by erosion, as sills or columns.

Lava dykes

Where lava has been forced up through cracks in the ground, it can solidify in the form of vertical lines or pipes. As surrounding, softer rock is eroded away, these dykes become exposed.

Tors

Tors are fascinating features that have captured people's imaginations through the ages. Often irregular in shape and figure-like in silhouette, many local tales have been spun to explain the origins of the strange towers of stone. Their real origins are more complex, but no less mysterious, as geologists are still discussing different theories as to how exactly they are formed. Tors often consist of igneous rocks, such as granite, or hard-wearing metamorphic rock, in temperate, periglacial and subtropical regions.

Tor origins

The granite tors on Dartmoor originated as igneous intrusions underground about 280 mya, during the Carboniferous period. One theory is that tropical conditions once contributed to the chemical breakdown of the rocks when they were located underground. The rocks were then exposed and dispersed in periglacial conditions by surface soil movement.

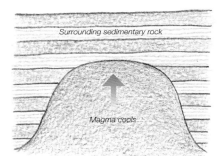

Surrounding sedimentary rock

Magma cools

Magma intrusion

The rock originates from the intrusion of molten magma deep underground millions of years ago. As the rock cooled, volatile gases and chemicals were trapped within it, eroding it along internal cracks.

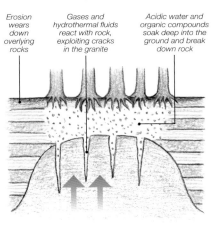

Tropical rainforest

Erosion wears down overlying rocks

Gases and hydrothermal fluids react with rock, exploiting cracks in the granite

Acidic water and organic compounds soak deep into the ground and break down rock

Breaking up

One theory suggests that erosion wears away the overlying rock and soil, allowing acidic water and organic chemicals from tropical rainforests to seep down into the rock and break it down.

Exploited rock vulnerable to breakdown and erosion by rainwater and ice

Cold climate

Another theory suggests that underground frost-shattering breaks down the rock in cold climates, and, when exposed, the rock is broken down further by rain, frost, and ice until it begins to fall apart.

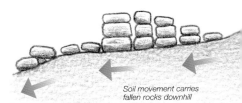

Soil movement carries fallen rocks downhill

Clitter and boulders

Erosion continues to batter the exposed rocks and exploit cracks. Surface soil movement in periglacial conditions carries the small, loose rocks downhill to scatter the boulders and stones that we see today.

Rock Crags & Ridges

Another form of rocky outcrop that you'll see in upland landscapes is a ridge, cliff or steep rocky escarpment. Again, these are made from much harder rocks than those that surround them and so they have been eroded more slowly, creating the protruding rock forms that we see today. Some ridges have been formed by very liquid magma that has flowed into horizontal cracks or joints between the surrounding rock, before solidifying. Other rocks such as some sandstones – for instance, millstone grit – have been formed under great pressures and have cemented to form harder, more competent rocks.

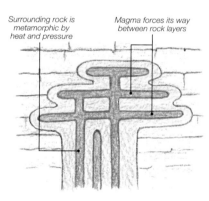

Surrounding rock is metamorphic by heat and pressure

Magma forces its way between rock layers

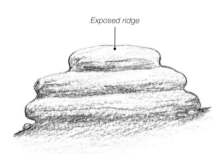

Exposed ridge

Transforming surrounding rock
When molten magma rises, it makes contact with large planes of the rock strata above and below, fusing with and transforming them under the intense heat and pressure before cooling.

Exposure of crag
Gradually, erosion wears down the ground above. Once the rock is exposed to the elements, the surrounding weaker rock breaks down and is eroded more quickly by rain, wind and ice to reveal the cliff or sill.

Sill on top

Some sills become impressive and important strategic features, such as Whin Sill across northern England, which the Romans used to their advantage when constructing Hadrian's Wall. Whin Sill is actually quite a complex form as the volcanic rock has been forced between and fused with the surrounding sedimentary rock.

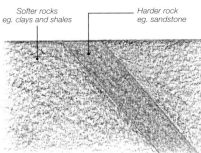

Softer rocks eg. clays and shales

Harder rock eg. sandstone

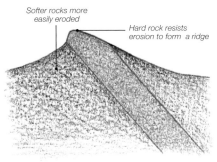

Softer rocks more easily eroded

Hard rock resists erosion to form a ridge

Sedimentation

Sediments of rock fragments are laid down in estuaries or lakes, or at coastlines. The layers pile on top of one another, the pressure building up on layers below, cementing and compacting some layers more than others.

Outcrop

Over time, the land is uplifted by tectonic movement, compressing and bending the layers of rock. The rock is eroded away and the more cemented, harder rock is worn away more slowly to reveal a rocky sandstone outcrop.

Loose Rock Faces

Wastwater screes
The dramatic scene at Wastwater in the Lake District in the north of England is heightened by the scree slopes, a great sweeping wall of rock fragments that have been broken away from the rock above by the action of frost.

Some steep mountain- or hillsides are covered in loose rock. These rock fragments have broken away over time as the solid rock above is broken down by the sun, rain, frost and ice. Rockslides and falls result, and the debris is carried down the slope by gravity. The results of these rock falls can be seen resting on the mountainside. These are known as screes or talus slopes, and they tend to be found at high altitudes, where the rock is exposed to severe weathering and erosion. Flat fields of loose rock, known as blockfields, are caused by frost action in periglacial conditions lifting the stones above ground.

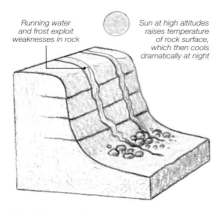

Running water and frost exploit weaknesses in rock

Sun at high altitudes raises temperature of rock surface, which then cools dramatically at night

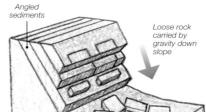

Rock slides

Angled sediments

Loose rock carried by gravity down slope

Rock breaks down

Exposed rock at high altitudes is subject to constant attack by extremes of temperature, which causes expansion and contraction, and the action of water, snow, ice and frost, all of which exploit weaknesses in the rock.

Rock falls

The composition and angle of rock sediments also play a role in how rock breaks away. Sometimes, large fragments break away along sloping planes of sediment, causing rockslides.

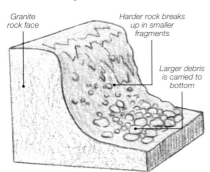

Granite rock face

Harder rock breaks up in smaller fragments

Larger debris is carried to bottom

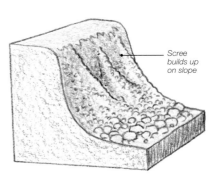

Scree builds up on slope

Debris collects

Rock that is more resistant to erosion breaks away in smaller fragments and falls down the slope to form scree, with the larger, heavier debris being carried to the bottom of the slope.

Scree slope forms

Scree builds up over time at the base of the slope and protects it from erosion. A lack of vegetation indicates that rock falls are still regular, so plants are unable to take root under the constant bombardment.

Hillside Terraces

Steps on the slope of a hillside, also known as 'terracettes', are one sign of the very slow, often imperceptible movement of soil down a slope called soil creep. Other signs include wrinkling or hummocks on hillsides. Soil and weathered rock on hillsides are always moving downhill under the influence of gravity, helped by the effects of moisture, frost and ice. This is why terracettes are more often seen on steep, soil-covered hillsides – in uplands and elsewhere – that are more prone to frost in damp or humid climates.

Terracettes
The terracettes on this hillside show the effects of soil creep. Ridges such as these can often be seen most clearly on steep, grazed grass slopes, where sheep and livestock have used the naturally occurring terraces to help them cross the hillside. The weight of the animals pushes down the earth and exaggerates the step effect.

Moisture and frost

Creep is caused by a number of factors, among them the action of moisture or frost. Soils containing clay particles absorb rainwater and release it when they dry, expanding and contracting as they do so, which causes them to move slightly downhill. Frost has a similar effect to rain. In upland areas prone to cold temperatures, the soil particles expand as they freeze. This raises them in a process called heave. When they thaw, they fall back, lower down the slope.

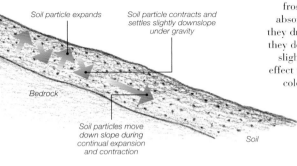

Soil particle expands

Soil particle contracts and settles slightly downslope under gravity

Bedrock

Soil particles move down slope during continual expansion and contraction

Soil

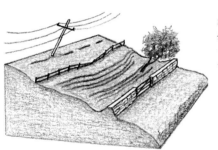

Waterlogged soil

Frozen soil

Terracettes

The soil's downward movement creates breakages in the surface of the ground. If there is only a thin layer of vegetation, the roots grip into the more solid rock or subsoil below, holding the top layer but creating ridges, often accentuated by the weight of grazing animals. Other signs of soil creep include the downward movement of tree trunks or man-made structures, such as poles or fences, or bulging walls where soil has been pushed against them.

Solifluction and gelifluction

In periglacial or cold upland regions, lower layers of soil can freeze solid. When the upper layers are warmed and thaw, the moisture is unable to drain; the top layer becomes fluid, causing it to flow downhill across the solid layers of soil or rock below, in a process called solifluction, creating lobes and terraces. This is slightly faster than soil creep. Gelifluction is a similar process that happens on top of permafrost – when the lower layers of soil are permanently frozen.

Earth & Rock Scars

More dramatic than terraces or other signs of soil creep are the scars in earth or rock hillsides caused by landslips or landslides. These are movements that happen much more quickly than soil creep. Sudden flows of large amounts of water down a hillside, as the result of a rainstorm or thaw of ice further up a mountainside, loosen the structure of the soil and add to its weight, carrying it downhill. Loose rock also falls suddenly, causing rockslides and falls. These earth and rock movements affect large areas of a hillside, shaping it over time.

Gone with the flow
The telltale scar in a hillside of a mudflow caused by water saturating the soil. Vegetation and small rocks have been carried down the slope in a stream of debris.

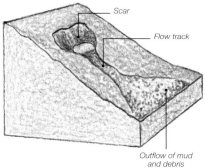

Scar

Flow track

Outflow of mud
and debris

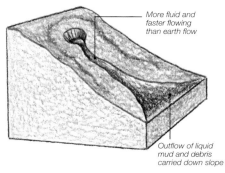

More fluid and
faster flowing
than earth flow

Outflow of liquid
mud and debris
carried down slope

Earth and mud flows

We've already seen how solifluction causes more rapid flows of earth than soil creep. Flows occur when clay-based soils on slopes are soaked and deformed and become semi-liquid. The soil flows downhill, causing flow tracks or bulging shapes in the ground known as lobes or tongues. Mud flows move more quickly as they have much higher water content. Mud flows leave long tracks of mud and small rocks.

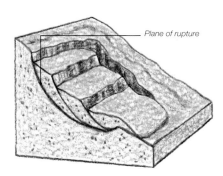

Plane of rupture

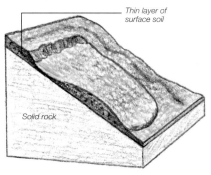

Thin layer of
surface soil

Solid rock

Landslides and slips

These are the sudden falls of large amounts of rock and soil down a hillside. A deep-seated landslide, such as a rotational landslide, involves a large unbroken mass of earth and/or rock moving along a deep plane of rupture. Shallow slips, also known as block or turf slides, occur where a superficial layer of surface material slides downhill across a rock layer. Slips create much smaller forms on the hillside.

Upland Rivers

Upland river
Fast-flowing rivers in uplands are at their most erosive in times of flood, when they are swollen by heavy rain or water from melting snow or glaciers, and can carry larger amounts of fragmentary material.

As we have seen in earlier pages, many mountain and upland features owe their existence and shapes to the existence of water following the easiest and quickest path downhill under the influence of gravity. Even the great valleys carved by glaciers – and the glaciers themselves – began life as streams and rivers. The effects of river erosion depend on the speed and amount of water flowing downhill – most erosion and transportation occurs during times of flood – and how resistant the underlying rock is to erosion.

Let it flow

Water from rain or melting snow and ice that does not evaporate back into the atmosphere runs down the mountainside and seeps into the ground. These streams begin at high velocity but low volume at the top of the mountain. The water carries rock and soil fragments, and together they shape the upland landscape over which they flow. Most transportation of debris and thus erosion occur, however, during short periods of heavy rainfall or melting ice, when much greater volumes of water flow downhill, carrying lots of debris. At several points water flowing above ground will be joined by groundwater – water that has seeped into the rock from higher up the valley and flows into streams and rivers from springs or emerging underground streams.

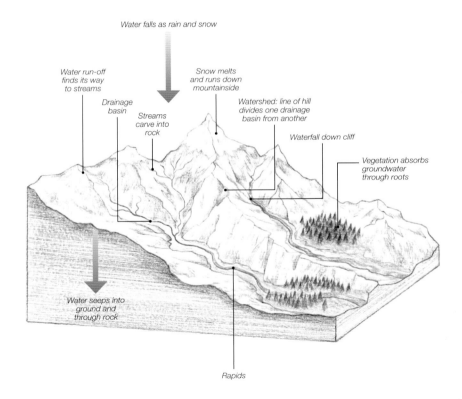

Water falls as rain and snow

Water run-off finds its way to streams

Drainage basin

Streams carve into rock

Snow melts and runs down mountainside

Watershed: line of hill divides one drainage basin from another

Waterfall down cliff

Vegetation absorbs groundwater through roots

Water seeps into ground and through rock

Rapids

Upland River Patterns

Lakeland rivers (right)
A map of the Lake District in Cumbria reveals that most of the river courses and their valleys lead away from the centre of the region in a radial pattern. This was caused by the uplift of the region by a large, igneous intrusion underground.

Looking at the patterns of rivers across an upland landscape can tell you a great deal about how that landscape came into being. If you look at the distribution and lines of the flow of rivers on a map, you will see that they follow the contours of the ground, which are mostly created by their own erosive action. However, their paths are also determined by the geology and history of the landscape, and so provide clues to the hardness of the underlying rocks and to how the landscape was formed.

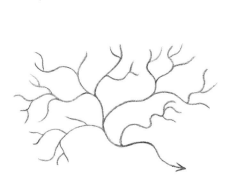

Dendron
Probably the most common type of river form, the rivers and their tributaries feed into each other in a tree-like pattern. This develops in areas with underlying rock that has the same resistance to erosion. One example of this is in Dartmoor in the UK.

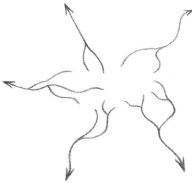

Radial
When the lines of streams and rivers radiate outwards from a centre, this indicates that the underlying ground has been uplifted into a dome-like shape, causing the rivers to carve valleys, such as in the Lake District, in Great Britain.

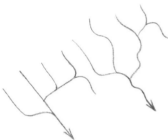

Trellis

A trellis network is formed when tributaries join rivers at right angles along weaknesses in the rock. This happens where the layers of rock are tilted to create blocks of differing resistance to erosion. The Ridge and Valley provinces of the Appalachians in the USA provide good examples.

Parallel

The simplest pattern of parallel rivers and tributaries tends to be found on recently uplifted slopes and ground of uniform resistance, where the water can flow downhill in streams along the same axis. This can be seen in some river patterns in Glen Fyne in Scotland, or the Appalachians.

Mountain Streams

Mountain stream
A mountain stream in the Lake District, UK. The small, slow-flowing stream has cut a narrow V-shaped gully in the hillside. Note how the rock and earth have been broken away in a small landslide near the stream's source, in what is known as headward erosion, probably during a succession of rain storms. Small rocks and boulders obstruct the flow of the stream, creating minor areas of turbulence and dissipating its destructive energy.

Found near the tops of mountains and hills, and often the humble source of a much larger river further downstream, mountain streams are usually minor and unobtrusive affairs. They are small and for most of the time are unable to carry large rocks or debris down the mountainside. This changes during heavy rainfall or when mountain-top glaciers, snow and ice thaw in spring, resulting in sudden deluges of large amounts of water and material with greater erosive power.

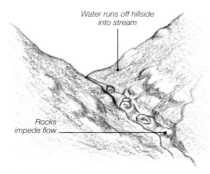

Water runs off hillside into stream

Rocks impede flow

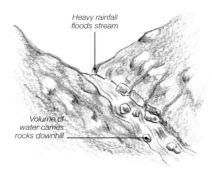

Heavy rainfall floods stream

Volume of water carries rocks downhill

Small beginnings

Rainwater runs off steep mountainsides or seeps underground to emerge as a spring. The small, slow-flowing streams are not capable of transporting large debris and have little erosive power.

Times of flood

During heavy rainfall, or in the spring when glaciers, snow and ice melt on the mountainside, large amounts of water suddenly soak the ground and run off down slopes, following the path of the stream.

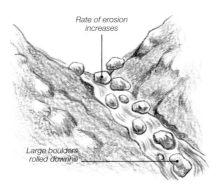

Rate of erosion increases

Large boulders rolled downhill

Feel the force

It is during these floods that the mountain stream suddenly gains velocity and ferocity, transporting much larger debris down the steep hillside, in turn breaking away large amounts of rock.

Downstream

Lower down the valleys, the streams meet up with other mountain streams, the combined flow creating larger upland rivers, with wider and deeper river beds, capable of transporting more material.

V-shaped Upland Valleys

V for valley
The distinctive V-form of an upland valley has been cut after many years of downward erosion. This process occurs mostly during times of flooding.

V-shaped upland valleys are formed when large rocks and boulders are washed downhill by torrents of flood water. Further downhill, the accumulation of rock debris in upland streams and rivers slows their flow for much of the time, creating winding channels in the hills. This changes when sudden and heavy flows of water increase the energy of the rivers and their ability to carry heavy rocks and stones, cutting V-shaped valleys in the landscape, which often wind between interlocking mounds called spurs.

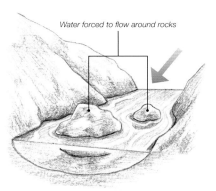

Water forced to flow around rocks

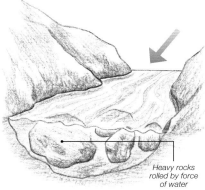

Heavy rocks rolled by force of water

Slowing the flow

Large boulders, which have been carried down the mountainside along streams during times of flood or from rock falls, line the river bottoms and obstruct the flow of the river, dissipating its energy.

Downcutting

During times of flood, however, the velocity and mass of the water are able to carry larger boulders and stones, rolling and bouncing them downstream. This action cuts downwards, creating a V-shaped valley.

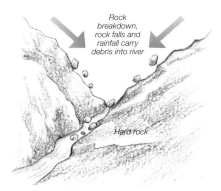

Rock breakdown, rock falls and rainfall carry debris into river

Hard rock

Taking the plunge

Heavy rainfall may cause earth and rock falls that shape valley sides. Where the rock is much more resistant to erosion but also permeable, such as limestone, the rivers may cut valleys with much steeper sides.

Winding on

The flow of rivers and the accumulation of debris cause the formation of meanders (see page 88), creating winding, turning upland river courses, that erode distinctive interlocking spurs through the hills.

Upland River Meanders

Rivers carve their way through the landscape to create V-shaped valleys but they rarely do so in a straight line. How river meanders begin to form is not clearly understood, but it is thought that they are caused by the natural pattern of water flow in a river. When rivers flood, the fast-flowing, swirling water picks up material and transports it to erode sequences of shallow, slower-flowing sections called riffles and deeper pools of fast-moving water, and gradually shaping regular bends.

Meanders

The rocks in this mountain stream have been deposited on the inside and crossover points between the bends in the stream in response to the flow of water. Where there is more debris, the water is shallower and becomes turbulent due to friction with the debris, while in the pools the water surface is flatter and smoother.

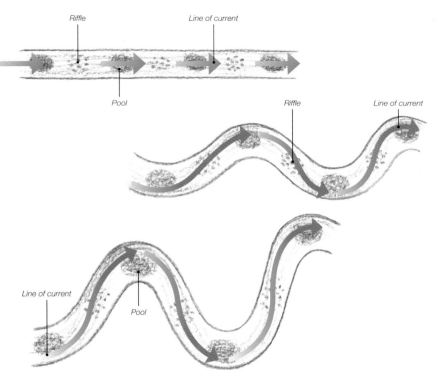

Riffle

Line of current

Pool

Riffle

Line of current

Line of current

Pool

Spiral flow

Upland streams and rivers tend to flow relatively slowly, with the large rocks and debris causing friction, slowing the water. When the volume of water increases during flood, more and heavier debris is carried, increasing the levels of erosion. As water flows downhill, it moves in the shape of a spiral or corkscrew, rising and falling and also swinging from side to side. This gradually creates a sequence of shallow, slow-moving stretches of water

and faster, more heavily eroded and deeper pools. The river picks up rocks and sediment in the faster-moving parts of the river, including from the outside of a gradually emerging bend, and carries them downstream where they cut into the river bed and bank. Where the flow of water slows and rises again, it deposits much of the debris on the inside of the next bend, building up a new bank. Over time, the flow of water and debris causes the bends in the river to widen.

River Islands

In times of flood, when rivers flow much faster, they are able to transport large loads of debris, including rocks, gravel, sand and sediment, which cut away at the landscape. As the flood subsides, the river is no longer able to lift the material and so it deposits it in large mounds, which partially obstruct its flow. This creates what are known as braided streams or rivers, which consist of multiple channels flowing around islands of deposits. These are commonly found in upland valley floors.

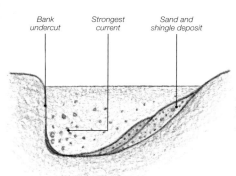

Bank undercut   Strongest current   Sand and shingle deposit

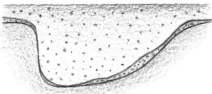

Banks

As meanders form, banks of debris, including pebbles, gravel and finer sediments, are deposited on the inside of bends and crossover points between bends.

Floods

During floods, when heavy rainfall or melting glaciers create large volumes of water, the debris is lifted and dispersed across the valley or carried downstream.

Debris island

This island of gravel in an Icelandic river has been deposited by floodwaters from the melting of snow and ice upstream. As the waters subsided, the river followed two new channels created either side of the island. It will take another flood to pick up the gravel and transport it further downstream.

Braiding

If the flood carries large amounts of debris, they build up into banks to block the flow of the water and divert the river into multiple, or braided, streams.

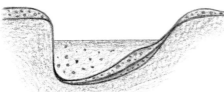

Islands

As the floodwaters recede, the river's velocity reduces, and the debris is deposited again in islands in the middle of the river flow, forcing the water to flow around them.

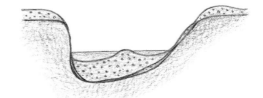

Waterfalls

Waterfalls are created when running water flows over a 'step' in the bedrock below. This can be caused when a crack opens up in the rock as a result of tectonic tension and the rock falls, creating a drop, or when a glacier carves into a valley side to create a hanging valley (see page 112). However, the most common form of waterfall is when water crosses from hard rock to softer rock, which erodes away more quickly, creating a deepening step. A drop in sea level can also increase the force of water flowing downwards, causing the rock to be eroded with new vigour in what is known as renewed downcutting.

Force flow
High Force in County Durham, northern England, demonstrates the capacity of a waterfall to cut through rock. The upper layers of rock, with vertical cooling joints, are the hard rock of Whin Sill (see page 73), while the lower horizontal bedding is the softer sedimentary rock, through which the water is cutting down and back.

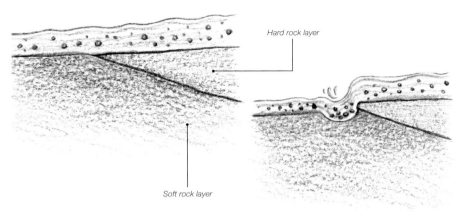

Hard rock layer

Soft rock layer

Hard to soft

As a river flows downhill it passes over rocks of varying hardnesses. At some points the water crosses from hard rock to softer rock. The debris being carried in the river erodes the softer rock, creating a step.

Stepping down

Erosion gradually cuts deeper into the soft rock, creating a larger step from the hard rock to the lower level. This increases the turbulence in the water, and the river scours a depression at the foot of the step.

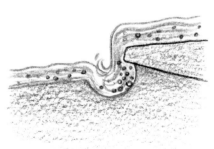

Taking the plunge

The waterfall cuts out a large indentation, known as a plunge pool, which catches and circulates the debris, cutting deeper into the soft rock layers and eroding it backwards, underneath the hard rock above.

Going back

Gradually, the undercutting weakens the harder layer of rock above and it crumbles and falls into the river. This repeated process causes the waterfall to continuously deepen and retreat upstream.

Rapids

Rapids differ from waterfalls in that they are characterised by a stretch of fast-flowing, turbulent water, rather than a single, tall step in gradient. They are formed where the downward slope of the river bed increases in steps, where the course of the river narrows, or where multiple obstacles, such as large boulders, line the river bed. Each of these factors increases the flow of the water as well as the turbulence and therefore the erosive force, as the water stirs up rock particles and batters them against the obstacles, river bed and neighbouring banks.

Turbulent flow
Rapids in Yoho National Park, in British Colombia, Canada, run with water flowing from melting glaciers high in the mountains. The extra turbulence created by the fast flow carves steps in the river, rather like small waterfalls.

Steps

As with waterfalls, some rapids are created by erosion cutting a series of steps down into the rock of the river bed, where layers of hard rock alternate with layers of softer rock. This disturbs the flow of the water.

Narrows

Sometimes large, durable outcrops of rock will stand in the way of the flow of the water, constricting its flow and creating areas of extreme turbulence as the water tries to flow through the narrower gap.

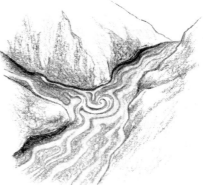

Boulders

Large boulders, possibly deposited by glaciers many years before and which are too heavy to be moved by the water or by floods, will also stand in the way of the water flow, creating turbulent currents.

Where two rivers meet

Rapids are also created when a fast-flowing river is joined by a fast-flowing tributary, particularly in times of flood. The increase in water flow and energy lead to greater erosion and steepening of the river bed.

Gorges

Very narrow, tall and steep-sided valleys or canyons are known as gorges. These are carved into rock by flowing water, and tend to be found where the rock is hard and resistant to erosion. This means that the debris carried by the water is limited in how much damage it can do to the surrounding rock, and so its force is concentrated directly below and in the direction of the flow of water. Gorges can be formed by erosion from flooding and waterfalls or the collapse of underground tunnels.

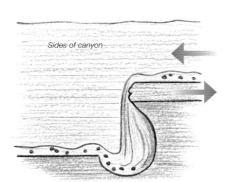

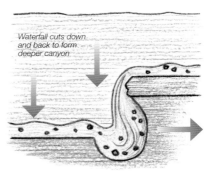

From waterfall to gorge
As we have seen, the formation of a waterfall is a continuous process. As the debris suspended in the water cuts away at the rock, lowering the fall of water, it is also eroding it backwards all the time.

The main force of the turbulent water is concentrated in the plunge pool below the point from which the water drops and against the back wall of the plunge pool, gradually cutting a channel down and back to create a deep, high-sided gorge.

Carved canyon

This side canyon, feeding the great Colorado River in the USA, has been carved by fast-flowing water, flooding at levels much higher than shown here, when the water is able to carry downstream larger rocks and debris that cut a channel down into the rock.

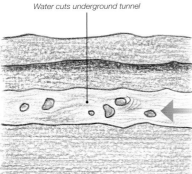

Water cuts underground tunnel

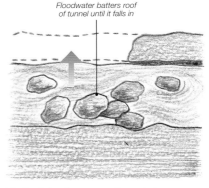

Floodwater batters roof of tunnel until it falls in

When the roof falls in

Where the rock is soft or permeable, such as limestone, water can seep underground. It erodes the rock away from underneath to form a tunnel, until the weakened rock roof collapses to form an open gorge.

Much of the damage to the rock in a gorge is done during sudden floods, when large amounts of water, released by heavy rainfall or melting snow and ice upstream, throw big boulders and debris against it in a headlong rush downstream.

Potholes

Potholes are distinctive features of fast-flowing upland rivers, streams and waterfalls. These are rounded shapes that you can find in solid rock or in large, immovable boulders over which water flows. They look as if they were made by the hand of humans, but the process that carves and polishes these hollows is water erosion at its most effective. Potholes can range in dimension from the size of a golf ball to the size of a truck.

Water hole
The smoothed, rounded sides of this pothole have been polished by the action of flowing water and loose stones.

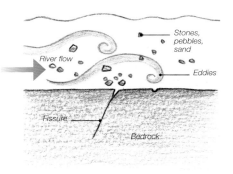

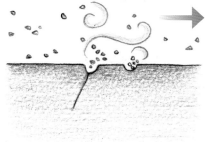

Fissures

Potholes are formed in a similar way to the much larger plunge pools in waterfalls. As water speeds across the river bed, it swirls over cracks or weaknesses in the rock.

Eddies

These turbulent eddies in the flowing water swirl hard rocks, pebbles, stones and sand against the cracks, wearing them open by loosening fragments in the cracks.

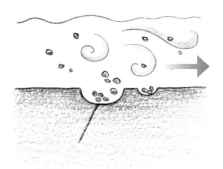

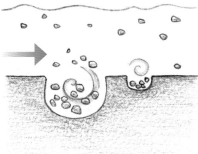

Hollowing out

Small stones and pebbles become trapped inside the holes that are formed. The movement of the swirling water inside the holes rubs the stones against rock.

Rounding off

The action of the stones smooths and rounds out the holes like polishing stones. Round stones can often be found still inside the potholes thus formed.

Debris Fans

Cone-like accumulations of debris, known as alluvial fans, are deposited at the base of steep hills and mountains by streams of water. They are mostly found in uplands in arid or cold climates where water flow is irregular and rare. In these areas when the rain falls or water from melting glaciers and ice flows downhill, it creates rivers of debris that deposit their load at the base of the valley.

Fan flow
This mound of silt, gravel and other fine debris on Spitsbergen, in the Arctic Circle, has been caused by a glacier meltwater stream running down the valley and reaching the more shallow gradient at the base of the mountains, where it has deposited all the material it carried. The dark streams of water at the right-hand base of the cone have fanned out into multiple channels.

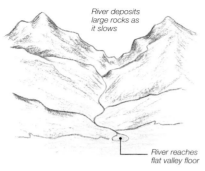

River deposits large rocks as it slows

River reaches flat valley floor

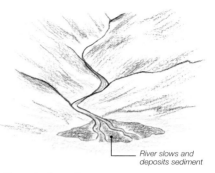

River slows and deposits sediment

Heavy load

Water carries rocks and earth particles down the valley from the mountainsides. As the river reaches more gradual gradients, it no longer has the power to carry the larger rocks and stones.

Down to the valley

The water carries the sediments to where the valley floor levels out, and here the water flow slows right down. The river outlet begins to deposit the sediment at the foot of the valley.

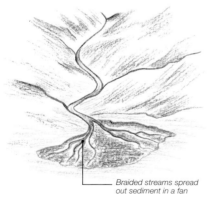

Braided streams spread out sediment in a fan

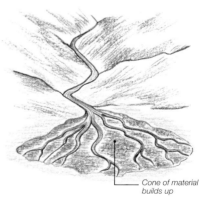

Cone of material builds up

Flowing out

Because of the flat, shallow gradient, the varying flow of water or landslides, the river disperses into braided streams – multiple rivulets flowing out in a fan from the base of the valley.

Rounding off

The streams of water deposit the sediment in a wide fan of material. This builds up over many years into a mound of fine material carried down the valley from the mountains upstream.

Glaciated Landscapes

Many regions that have experienced cold temperatures have been shaped by the huge forces exerted by ice. Glaciers are formed by the accumulation and compaction of snow year on year during cold periods, when it fails to melt during the summer. The snow first collects in hollows and the highest parts of valleys and then builds up and hardens into large masses of 'plastic' ice that flow very slowly downhill under the influence of gravity, carving out great gaps in the mountains. During the last ice age, around 18,000 years ago, glaciers covered large parts of northern Europe and America as well as South America and New Zealand.

Mark of a glacier
The Garschen Valley in the Swiss Alps is typical of a glaciated valley, with a broad, flat floor and sides that rise in a U shape.

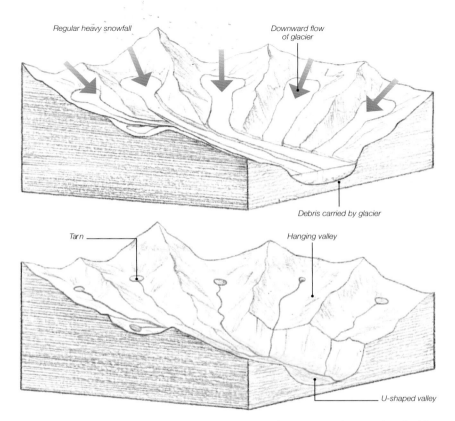

Regular heavy snowfall

Downward flow of glacier

Debris carried by glacier

Tarn

Hanging valley

U-shaped valley

During and after glaciation

A glacier forms when more snow is created year on year than is able to melt. The pressure that is created by large amounts of snow melts some of it, and then the water refreezes and recrystallises where there is less pressure. The ice crystals gradually become smaller and start interlocking, creating a movable mass. The ice is more brittle at the surface, but lower down the ice particles are more plastic and malleable. Flow occurs within the crystals and also as they rotate or slide past each other. Gravity acts on the mass of heavy ice to carry it downhill. Glaciers erode the rock to leave their marks on the landscape. Also, a glacier continuously melts at its front, releasing water and debris, and this leaves behind characteristic features on the landscape.

Mountain Basins

A round, bowl-shaped basin, nestling high above a valley between jagged mountain peaks and often filled by a small lake or tarn, marks the birthplace of a valley's glacier and the principal source of the erosion that carved much of the valley below. These hollows at the top of glaciated valleys, called cirques by geologists (also called cwms in Wales and corries in Scotland), are where the snows began to accumulate that ultimately gave rise to the glacier that eventually flowed down into the valley.

Snowdon cirque
The summit of Mount Snowdon, in north Wales, overlooks Lake Glaslyn, which occupies a circular basin carved by glacial ice. The lake is dammed at its open side by a lip of rock that was not fully eroded by the action of the glacier.

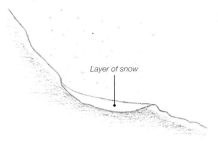

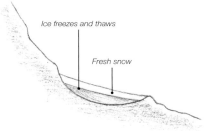

First snows

When snow begins to fall heavily, it first collects in previously eroded hollows, particularly on the shaded and sheltered sides of mountains. The layers of snow gradually build up and compress.

Freeze and thaw

Some ice melts during warm periods and then refreezes when the climate cools again. The meltwater and the expansion and contraction of the ice cause the rock to break apart, and debris falls into the ice.

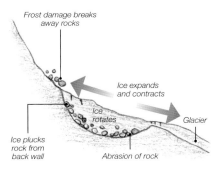

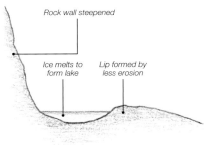

Going round

Pieces of detached rock under the ice and the action of freezing and thawing rotates the ice, grinding the ice-encased rocks against the underlying surface, creating a hollowed-out bowl in the rock.

Tarn time

The ice eventually recedes. A 'lip' is formed at the mouth of the cirque by the reduction in erosive force at this point. The ice melts in the hollow to create a tarn. Cirques are probably formed over several ice ages.

Mountain Peaks & Edges

Pyramidal peak
Neighbouring cirque glaciers can carve the rock to 'sharpen' it into knife-like edges. They carved the flat-sided peak, or horn, of the Matterhorn, which lies on the Swiss/ Italian border.

Some of the most dramatic mountains have been ground by the action of glaciers into the shapes that we see today. Sharp, jagged edges that run along the tops of mountains, and tall pyramid-like peaks with three or more vertical, planed sides, owe their forms to the large volumes of ice that accumulated in mountain regions. Between the peaks often lie sharp ridges, which are known as arêtes, an example of which is Striding Edge in the Lake District in the north of England.

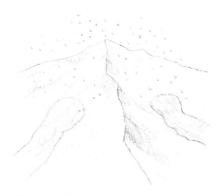

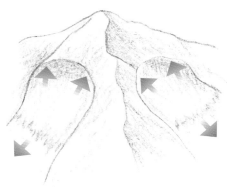

Cirque circle

As seen on page 104, snow collects at the top of mountains to form ice in hollows that gradually accumulates and erodes circular bowls. Sometimes, several of these indentations develop close together.

Plucky ice

As the glaciers build up, the actions of freezing and thawing and abrasion break down and 'pluck out' fragments from the rock surface, deepening and enlarging the hollow backwards.

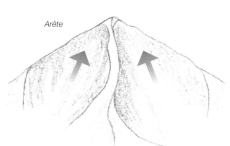

Arête

Horn

Come together

Over time, the ice carves out steep slopes in the mountain's side. Where two glaciers meet from neighbouring valleys or cirques, they create a sharp top edge along the ridge, also known as an arête.

Round the horn

Where three or more glaciers meet, they carve out pyramid-like peaks called horns, with steep, nearly vertical sides. Some famous and distinctive mountain peaks have been formed in this way.

U-shaped Valleys

Valleys that were shaped by glaciers often retain a distinctive U profile when viewed head-on, and are therefore the most obvious sign that the region was shaped by glaciation at some time. These valleys have steep sides, a flat bottom, and are usually straighter than if the valleys were simply formed by water erosion. A small stream or river often winds down the centre of the valley, flowing over and around the rock debris that was deposited when the ice finally melted away.

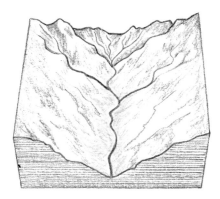

From V to U
All glaciated valleys begin life as river-eroded valleys. As seen on page 86, running water slowly carves a V-shaped valley down the mountainside.

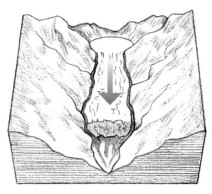

Ice flow
As the ice age takes hold, heavy snow falls first at the top of the valley (see page 102), gradually creating a large mass of glacial ice. The ice slowly flows downhill.

Valley deep

The steep sides of Yosemite Valley, in the USA, rise high above the flattened floor below in a U shape. Glaciers have eroded the valleys several times during the last two to three million years.

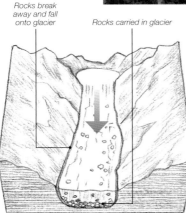

Rocks break away and fall onto glacier

Rocks carried in glacier

Scouring the valley

The moving ice plucks rock from the mountainside and transports it down the valley. Lumps of rock become lodged in the ice and scour the valley floor and sides.

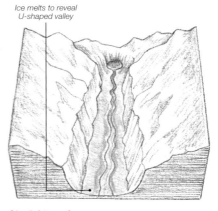

Ice melts to reveal U-shaped valley

Glacial trough

The ice recedes to leave what is known as a glacial trough, with steeply sloping sides and a flat valley bottom, although the shape also depends on the resistance of the rock.

Fjords

Fjord

The spectacular Geirangerfjord on the northwestern coast of Norway is one of the world's most visited fjords. The glacier cut a huge chasm through the rock, creating hanging valleys and waterfalls.

Perhaps the most impressive of all the landscape forms created by the actions of glaciers, fjords are huge, partially submerged valleys that are open to the sea. These massive coastline features are characterised by tall, sheer sides that descend deep into the water below. Fjords are found in formerly glaciated mountain regions that border the sea. They can be found along the west coasts of Norway and Greenland, and in some parts of North America, as well as in New Zealand and South America.

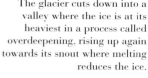

Original valley floor

Sea

Overdeepening

The glacier cuts down into a valley where the ice is at its heaviest in a process called overdeepening, rising up again towards its snout where melting reduces the ice.

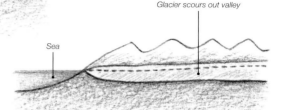

Glacier scours out valley

Sea

Glacial erosion

Fjords are created in the same way as other glaciated valleys, but next to the sea. Glaciers build up during an ice age as the sea level drops by up to 130m (425ft) or so.

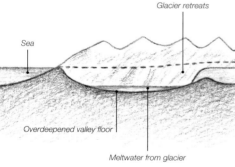

Glacier retreats

Sea

Overdeepened valley floor

Meltwater from glacier

Shallow mouth

Fjords tend to be shallower at their mouths because of overdeepening and because debris was carried there by the glacier. Deposits also collect at the mouth of the fjord.

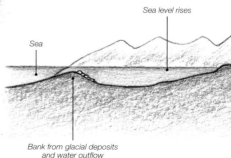

Sea level rises

Sea

Flooding

A subsequent rise in temperatures, ending the ice age, causes the glaciers to melt away and the sea level to rise, flooding the valley, and creating the fjord.

Bank from glacial deposits and water outflow

Hanging Valleys

Just hanging
The Bridalveil Falls waterfall pours from a hanging valley into the main glaciated valley in Yosemite National Park, USA. The hanging valley sides have been shaved off to create the sheer cliffs.

Sometimes, side or tributary valleys that feed into a large glacier-eroded valley are higher than the main valley floor. These side valleys are known as hanging valleys, and were formed when a larger glacier cut down further than the tributary glaciers in the side valleys. Often an accompanying feature of hanging valleys, truncated spurs are where the ridges between the tributary valleys have been 'chopped' or shortened by a passing glacier.

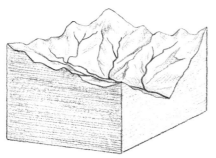

Ice erosion

A valley and its tributaries are gradually created by water erosion. A prolonged period of cold weather brings glaciers that follow the same courses as the river valleys.

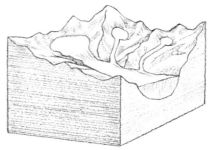

Deeper and down

Over time, the main valley is eroded more deeply and more quickly than the tributary valleys as a result of the greater erosive power of the much larger main glacier.

Waterfall

The ice recedes to reveal the hanging valleys along the sides of the main valley, often with their river courses ending as waterfalls dropping into the valley below.

Deepening

The main valley is deepened further over time as the glacier grows in mass from continued snowfall.

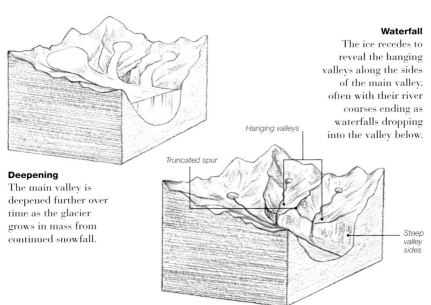

Hanging valleys

Truncated spur

Steep valley sides

Smoothed & Carved Rocks

Another sign of glacial erosion in a valley are the large rocks that have been rounded and smoothed and often show large parallel grooves, striations and cracks, all running in the direction of the valley. These marks have been cut by the stones and gravel that were dragged across the rocks by the glacier as it passed over them. The movement of the ice over large outcrops also creates features known as roches moutonnées, or sheep rocks, and 'crag and tail' outcrops.

Rocks fall onto glacier from above

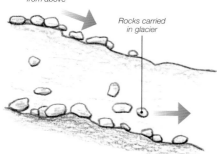

Rocks carried in glacier

Rocks dragged over outcrop

Scratches and grooves
The glacier carries along debris of varying sizes, dragging it across the underlying rock, and scrapes grooves and scratches across the rock's surface.

Smooth going
Where the underneath of the glacier encounters large, prominent rock outcrops, it smooths and polishes them on the side facing the direction of flow.

Smooth rock

This large rock in the Morteratsch glacial valley in Switzerland has been smoothed and rounded by stones and ice being dragged along the valley floor on the bottom of a glacier.

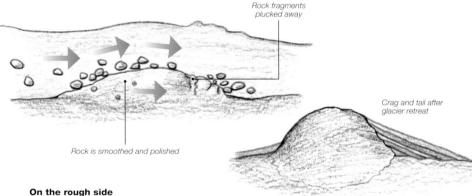

Rock fragments plucked away

Rock is smoothed and polished

Crag and tail after glacier retreat

On the rough side

On the side facing away from the flow, the changes in pressure in the ice cause it to thaw and refreeze on the rock, breaking it up to create the shape of a sheep rock, or roche moutonnée.

Crag and tail

Large volumes of rock and debris may be deposited on the other side of very large outcrops of rock as the glacier flows past, creating a 'crag and tail' feature, such as Castle Crag in Edinburgh, Scotland.

Banks & Mounds

Rock row
Features that appear in today's landscape as large banks and mounds were once rows of rock fragments and other deposits left by the a glacier's melting ice. They eventually become overgrown with vegetation.

A glacier is constantly thawing and refreezing as it moves down a valley. As the ice melts, glaciers deposit lots of debris called till, ranging from large rocks to fine materials, such as sand and clay, in piles, banks or lines. These piles of debris are called moraines and may sometimes initially look like lines of exposed rocks. However, often the deposits include a lot of fine sediment, so grass and vegetation grow on them and they look like banks or mounds lying in lines across or along the valley floor.

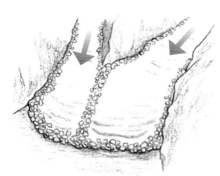

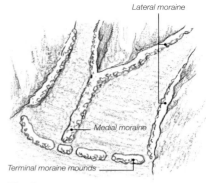

Lateral moraine

Medial moraine

Terminal moraine mounds

Breaking away

Rock fragments break off from the sides of a valley or are plucked away by the action of the glacier. The debris – which consists of a range of material from large boulders to fine sediment – is then carried down the valley on and in the ice, in lines of material along the sides, base and in the middle of the glacier.

Moraines

When the ice melts, it is no longer competent enough to be able to carry all the debris. This unsorted debris of all types and sizes is deposited in banks along the sides (as lateral moraines), middle (medial moraines, where two glaciers meet) and across the valley where the glacier stopped (terminal moraine).

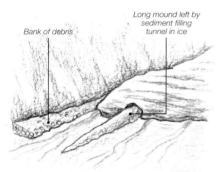

Long mound left by sediment filling tunnel in ice

Bank of debris

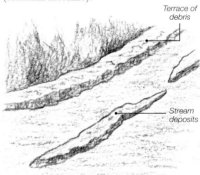

Terrace of debris

Stream deposits

Meltwater banks

As a glacier melts, streams flow between the side of the glacier and the valley wall. The streams leave behind material that forms banks when the glacier has gone.

Eskers

Other linear banks, called eskers, can be formed by streams flowing through tunnels under the glacier. The banks remain when the glacier melts.

Large Rocks & Boulders

Boulder (right)
A large boulder in Snowdonia in Wales. The obvious differences between some boulders and the rock beneath them led to them being called erratics.

We've seen how a valley can be carved by the rock fragments and debris that are transported by a glacier in motion. As the glacier melts, it begins to dump some of the material it carries – loose rocks, boulders and sediment. Some of the large rocks and boulders are deposited on the scenery as conspicuous features in the landscape, standing out not only because of their size but because they are of a different type of rock from that below and around them. Note that many large boulders can also fall onto a valley floor from the slopes above as a result of earth movement caused by melting permafrost.

Rock fragments
A glacier plucks fragments of stone from the rock face by melting into the rock's cracks and weaknesses and refreezing. As the mass of ice flows on, it rips the rock away.

Carried away
Rocks also fall from the slopes above onto the ice or into fissures in the glacier and are carried along, sometimes dropping further into the ice as it thaws and refreezes.

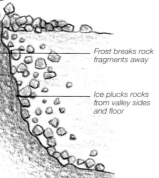

Frost breaks rock fragments away

Ice plucks rocks from valley sides and floor

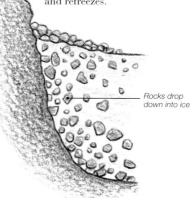

Rocks drop down into ice

Lateral moraine

Smoothed boulders
deposited on valley floor

Deposited rocks

When the ice melts, its density reduces
so it can no longer carry the debris that
has become lodged inside it. The rocks are
deposited at the bottom of the glacier,
where they can be dragged along further or
are left behind when the glacier retreats.

Small Rounded Hills

Glacial deposits can also take the form of small, low, elongated hills that can be found lying across glaciated plains. These can be very hard to distinguish from other forms of hill, but they are usually found in large groups, and can be distinguished because they all 'point' in the direction of the original ice flow. Although there is still a lot of discussion about exactly how these hills are formed, they are thought to be the result of material being dumped by glaciers partially melting and then moving over the piles of deposits thereby shaping them.

Drumlin hill
Small, rounded hills, called drumlins by geologists, are very hard to tell from hills formed by other means, or even old spoil heaps from mining. They often have a rounded, egg-shaped appearance and are usually found in groups, with each hill oriented along the same axis.

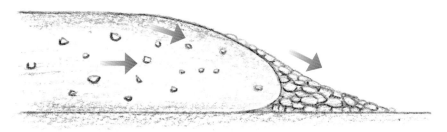

Depositing material

A glacier is constantly partially thawing and refreezing, depositing rocks and sediment in piles under the ice sheet, as it moves forwards under the force of gravity and as snow and ice subside and accumulate.

Shaping mounds

The piles of rock and sediment deposits are smoothed by the ice as the glacier passes over them. This creates large, rounded mounds, sometimes with large rocks at their centre surrounded by finer till.

Drumlins

After the glacier has retreated, large, egg-shaped forms, or drumlins, are left behind, often in groups called fields. The 'pointed' ends of the hills all point in the direction of the glacier's flow.

Hummocks

Hummocky ground
Glaciers sometimes leave signs of melting ice behind in the form of undulating terrain, with small hills, banks and hollows. The holes often fill up with water and vegetation.

As well as mounds, banks and hills, another feature that glacial deposition can leave behind is a large area of uneven ground, with a range of hollows and hummocks. These are thought to be another type of moraine, consisting of rocks, sand and gravel that have been carried along by a glacier in crevices and folds in the ice sheet and then deposited on the ground as the glacier receded. Sometimes, the hollows between the mounds fill with water, like kettle lakes (see page 124), or become clogged up with vegetation to form boggy patches.

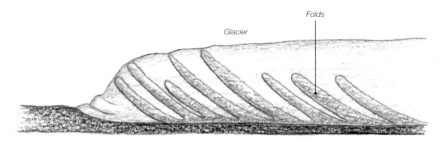

Ice faults and folds

An active glacier is constantly thawing and refreezing as it moves forwards. This means that areas of melted ice inside the glacier are compressed, stretched, split and folded in the same way as rock behaves under pressure.

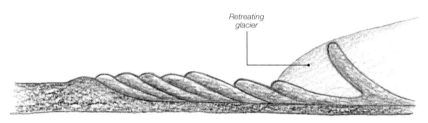

Deposits

Sediment and rocks are carried in these thrusts and folds in the ice, so when the glacier eventually melts and recedes, they become deposited on top of each other in a succession of mounds and layers, forming the hummocks.

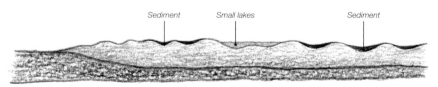

Hummocks

These mounds are gradually eroded by rain and sometimes in-filled with water and more sediments as meltwater flows from the thawing glacier. This leaves behind the irregular terrain of hummocks that we see in the landscape today.

Small Low-lying Lakes

Mainly found in flat, low-lying areas that have been glaciated, kettle lakes can also be found in upland areas. As with hummocks, these features usually consist of a group of round hollows that are sometimes scattered across the ground and are often filled with water to form circular lakes. Kettle lakes are created by blocks of ice that break away from the melting glacier. Over time, the holes may become clogged up with silt and vegetation to form patches of bog or marsh in the valley floors.

Kettle lakes
These kettle lakes were formed in the wake of a retreating glacier in North Dakota, USA.

Retreating glacier

Block of ice breaks away

Blocks of ice

As the glacier melts and retreats, large blocks of ice detach from its front, along with the sediment and debris deposited by the streams of meltwater.

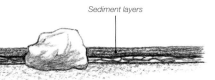

Sediment layers

Sediment build-up

The solid block of ice takes a while to melt completely. In the meantime, sediment deposited by meltwater surrounds the ice, building up in layers around it.

Meltwater and rainwater

Melting the ice

As the block of ice melts, it leaves a circular hole in the surrounding sediments, which partially subside into the crater. Meltwater and rainwater fill the hole.

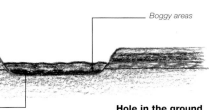

Boggy areas

Vegetation and water

Hole in the ground

Several blocks of ice create a group of small lakes or an undulating landscape of mounds and hollows. Vegetation and water may fill the holes to create boggy areas.

Long Lakes

Blue ribbon (right)
Blue ribbon (right)
Loch Avon winds
along the bottom
of the U-shaped,
glaciated Glen Avon
in the Scottish
Highlands. The
centre of the valley
floor was scraped
out by the glacier
in a process of
overdeepening.

Glaciated valleys may contain long, winding lakes that sit
in depressions in the valley floor. These depressions have
been scraped out by the erosive force of the glacier. We
have already seen how glaciers can overdeepen a valley
(see page 111), and these indentations subsequently
become filled with water. A lake can also form in the floor
of a valley when a moraine left by a glacier creates a dam
across the width of the valley.

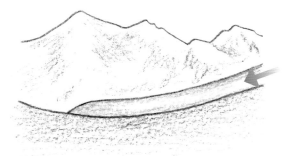

Shallowing
The reduction in the amount
of ice near the front of the
glacier means that the
glacier does not hollow out
the rock as much, leading to
a shallower profile.

Hollowing out
As explained previously
(see page 100), the
bottom of a fjord is
hollowed out by the
action of a glacier. As
a glacier makes its way
down the valley, the
weight of the ice abrades
the valley floor.

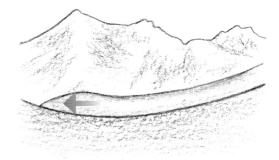

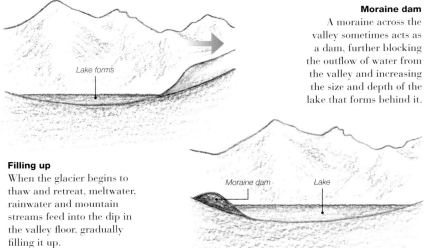

Moraine dam

A moraine across the valley sometimes acts as a dam, further blocking the outflow of water from the valley and increasing the size and depth of the lake that forms behind it.

Filling up

When the glacier begins to thaw and retreat, meltwater, rainwater and mountain streams feed into the dip in the valley floor, gradually filling it up.

Introduction

Lowland areas may, on the surface, appear less dramatic than upland landscapes but they have been subject to the same processes and are sometimes as complex in their structure as their mountainous counterparts. Of course, some of the landforms we explored in uplands can also occur in lowland areas, but the plains and softly undulating hills of low-lying landscapes also exhibit particular characteristics of their own.

Reed bed

Marsh

Estuary

The low-down

Lowland landscapes are characterised by their low-relief, often gently undulating hills, as well as by wide, sweeping plains and fast-flowing, wide rivers that run down to the sea. As the gradients of the landscape and rivers reduce, so rivers begin to shed their load, and many features in lowland landscapes are created by the resulting process of deposition. Thus the ground in lowland areas is often composed of layers of deposited sediment carried down from the uplands. Other features of lowlands include wetlands, such as floodplains, marshes, reedbeds, bogs and fens, often lining lowland valley floors, particularly in temperate and tropical climates. Large dry saltflats and sands are often characteristic of lowlands in arid areas.

Lowland features
Lowland landscapes are the most heavily populated areas on Earth because of their rich natural resources. Flood plains provide rich nutrients for farming and the rivers that deposited the nutrients provide fresh water for consumption and transport.

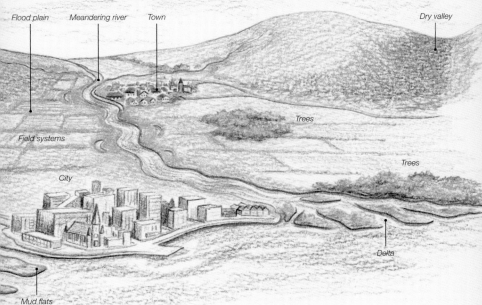

Flood plain

Meandering river

Town

Dry valley

Trees

Field systems

Trees

City

Delta

Mud flats

Lowland Hills & Valleys

In much the same way as their upland counterparts, low-relief hills and valleys are formed by a combination of uplift, folding, erosion and deposition. But while many uplands are formed of durable rock, lowland areas often consist of layers of much softer rocks, such as limestones, shales and clays. These consist of fine sediments deposited by slow-moving water, which are then bent as plates crush against each other and worn down by erosive forces.

Ups and downs
The South Downs of Sussex in England are formed from a number of layers of limestone sediment laid down by ancient seas. The texture and consistency of the chalk means that the layers have been eroded over millions of years to form the soft, rolling shapes of the South Downs that we see today.

Anatomy of a lowland landscape

The rolling hills of the Weald of southeast England demonstrate how a lowland landscape has been shaped over millions of years. The rocks were laid down in the form of silt, sand and mud in ancient lakes and seas between 125 and 90 mya, and then as soft white limestone seabeds (chalk) until about 65 mya. The layers of compacted sediment hardened into rock layers, which were then uplifted and bent into an elongated dome by the collision of the European and African plates around 20 mya. Since then, the layers of chalk have been eroded to expose the lower layers of clay and sandstone in the valleys, leaving chalk ridges at the highest points of the North and South Downs.

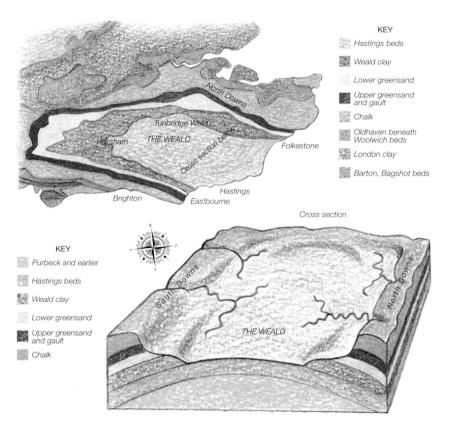

KEY
- Hastings beds
- Weald clay
- Lower greensand
- Upper greensand and gault
- Chalk
- Oldhaven beneath Woolwich beds
- London clay
- Barton, Bagshot beds

KEY
- Purbeck and earlier
- Hastings beds
- Weald clay
- Lower greensand
- Upper greensand and gault
- Chalk

Cross section

Dry Valleys

Some lowland valleys appear to have been eroded by a river and yet there is no trace of one lying in the bottom of the valley. So how were these valleys shaped? Dry valleys are commonly found in limestone landscapes, including chalk downland, and in some porous sandstones. These rocks are permeable, allowing water to seep down through them, which means that the valley shape we see today was created with the help of other factors some time in the landscape's past. There are several explanations.

Running dry

Dry valleys are often formed during periglacial conditions, when permafrost has frozen permeable rock, such as limestone, so that it becomes for a time impermeable. Any water that runs over the rock is unable to seep into the ground. When the climate warms, water is once again able to permeate the ground, leaving dry valleys.

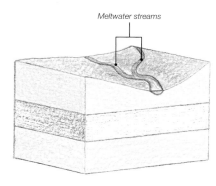

Meltwater streams

Colder climates

If the landscape has been subject to prolonged, very cold periods, the normally permeable rock would have been frozen to substantial depths by the permafrost, making the upper layers of the rock impermeable to the flow of water.

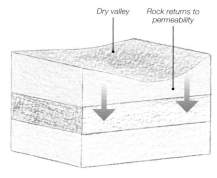

Dry valley *Rock returns to permeability*

Valley erosion

Any water would have run off the surface of the rock, creating valleys by erosion. When temperatures rose, and the layers of rock returned to permeability, the water could seep down into the rock again and its erosive action would be discontinued.

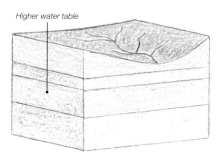

Higher water table

More water

The temporary re-emergence of small streams at the bottom of dry valleys after heavy downpours indicates that periods of heavy rainfall during wetter climatic conditions may have caused the original erosion of the valley floor.

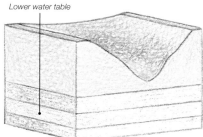

Lower water table

Lower water table

Another hypothesis suggests that present-day water tables are much lower than in the past because of higher water extraction for agriculture, for instance. Therefore surface water flows would have been more common in the past.

Isolated Hills

Exposed outcrop (right)

This granite outcrop, known locally as a kopje, rises above the Serengeti plains in Tanzania. It provides a sheltered habitat for many plants and animals.

Some lowland landscapes feature an isolated hill, rock or small mountain that stands above the surrounding low-lying ground. While these prominent outcrops are sometimes harder than surrounding rock, they are all that remains of higher ground after many years of erosion by water, wind and ice. These remaining, residual hills are the ones that lie furthest away from river courses, and therefore were the least exposed to erosion in times of flood.

New ground

A newly formed or uplifted area of rock is immediately subject to erosion by rain and running water. Rivers begin to erode courses into the rock's surface.

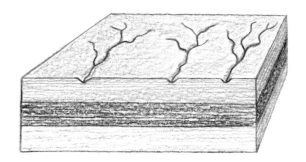

Hills and valleys

As the rivers erode into the ground, they create deep valleys and ranges of hills, with very little of the original surface of the rock remaining.

Plain

After very many years of erosion, a few low-lying isolated hills or outcrops of rock remain, surrounded by open flat ground, known as a peneplain.

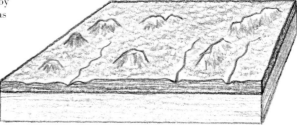

Lowland Rivers

As a river flows down to the sea, following the gradient of the land down to sea level, it carries the debris eroded in its upper reaches further downstream. By the time the river reaches low-lying areas, the material suspended or carried in the water exists in the form of much finer sediments, such as sand and silt. These sediments are then deposited when the river slows and floods, creating expansive, flat areas bordering the river.

Fertile plains
The River Severn winds across a heavily farmed plain in the UK. Over the years, the river has deposited layers of nutrient-rich sediments across the floodplain, making the area a fertile landscape suitable for farming.

On the level

As rivers flow downhill from upland regions to lower areas levelled by erosion, the gradient of the rivers lessens. The rivers meander through lowland regions, winding from side to side, cutting flat, wide valleys. The rivers slow and widen, depositing the debris that they are carrying across the flat floodplains through which they pass. These meandering rivers turn into braided rivers or deltas, slowing further in lakes or marshland, and widening out into estuaries or mudflats as they reach the sea. On their way to the sea, some rivers meander through arid regions but their sources are invariably to be found in neighbouring wet or mountainous areas.

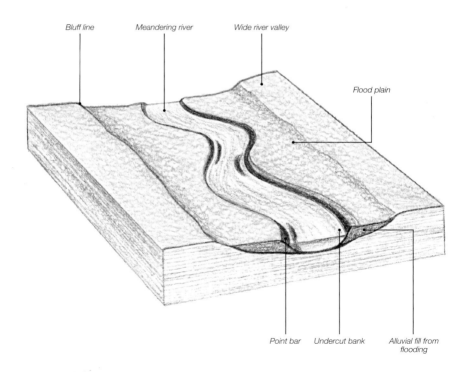

Bluff line

Meandering river

Wide river valley

Flood plain

Point bar   Undercut bank   Alluvial fill from flooding

Springs

Many rivers are served by springs (which occur in both lowland and upland areas). The presence of a spring depends on the level of the water table underground. As rainwater drains into the ground it fills up available space in the rock below, seeping between the cracks in the rock and saturating permeable rock and soil. The point below which the underground material is completely saturated is known as the water table. Springs occur where the water leaks above ground.

Small beginnings
The source of the great River Seine that flows through France rises in a cave and collects in this pond near Saint-Seine-l'Abbaye. The water drains into a stream which eventually becomes the Seine.

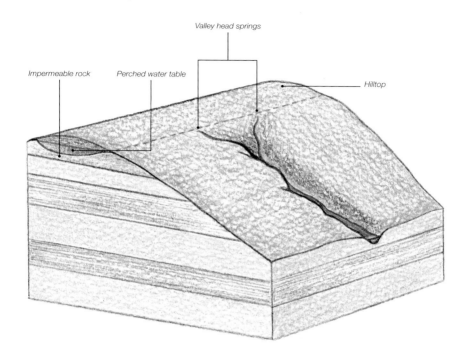

Valley head springs

Impermeable rock   Perched water table

Hilltop

Spring sources

The level of the water table depends on the amount of rainfall and the porosity of the rock below ground. Where a layer of permeable rock lies above impermeable rock on a hillside, water will seep down, but then flow underground along the top of the impermeable rock. This creates what is known as a perched water table. The groundwater will then re-emerge at the ground surface at the junction between the two types of rock. Many valley head springs flow from these perched water tables, providing the sources for rivers that flow downhill, creating valleys by erosion.

Rivers & Oxbows

Winding river
The Blackfoot River in Montana, USA, winds its way across marshy floodplains. Its ever-changing course has created multiple channels and oxbow lakes.

On page 88, we explored how rivers begin to adopt the curved meander shape familiar in many valleys. When rivers reach broad lowland plains, the dynamics of the water flow create winding S bends across wide river valleys and floodplains. These bends gradually widen and move in the direction of the water flow, creating particular patterns of erosion and deposition.

Widening

As erosion progresses, the bends slowly move downstream. At the same time, as the river meets the sides of the valley, it erodes them, widening the valley.

Moving on

When a river reaches lowland plains, it uses as much energy in transporting material as in erosion, but it gently cuts into its river banks to create curving S bends.

Oxbows

Flooding causes the river to overflow and cut off the main bend of the meander, creating a new channel and leaving behind an 'oxbow' lake or pool.

Marshes

Over time, the wandering course of the river leaves oxbow lakes and indentations in the valley floor which become marshy areas that are attractive to wildlife.

Floodplains

Water world (right)
The River Severn swamps the fields near Tewkesbury in Gloucestershire, UK. The flooding river has reached the edges of the slightly higher ground either side of the floodplain.

Floodplains are the large, flat areas that border rivers in lowlands and are susceptible to being covered in water when the river floods. They are gradually created by the processes of erosion and deposition as the river intermittently floods. The large amounts of nutrient-rich silt that floods deposit across these areas make them very fertile and ideal for farming and settlement, although there is severe disruption to the population when floods occur.

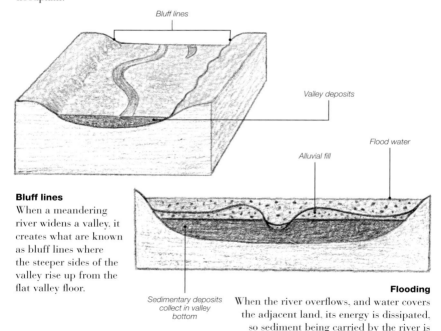

Bluff lines

Valley deposits

Flood water

Alluvial fill

Bluff lines
When a meandering river widens a valley, it creates what are known as bluff lines where the steeper sides of the valley rise up from the flat valley floor.

Sedimentary deposits collect in valley bottom

Flooding
When the river overflows, and water covers the adjacent land, its energy is dissipated, so sediment being carried by the river is deposited across the valley floor.

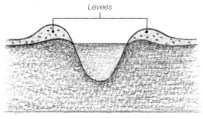

Levees

Coarse, heavy material is deposited first, to create riverside banks or levees. The finer sediments are carried further away from the river across the floodplain.

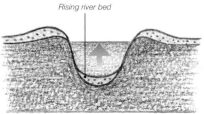

Raised river bed

As the flood subsides, the water within the channel deposits more material on the river bed, raising the river and increasing the chance of the river flooding its banks again.

River Terraces

LOWLANDS

Off the shelf
The shelf-like ledges that line the side of the Tsarab river, in the Indian Himalayas, indicate the previous levels of the river and the floodplain.

River valleys with meandering rivers and floodplains sometimes include naturally formed, broad, flat terraces that lie apart from the river course but also follow the line of the valley. These river terraces can be created in two ways. The first involves the river altering its meandering course over time, and the second is caused by a period of renewed downcutting by the river.

Terraces

The river's meanders continue to cut sideways across the valley floor, away from the old bank, and a terrace appears. If the process is repeated, it creates a succession of terraces along the side of the valley.

Wandering scar

Terraces are formed as a river gradually cuts into its valley. Variations in the flow of water and in the sediment load in the river, as a result of changes in climate, cause the river to change its course and the floodplain moves accordingly.

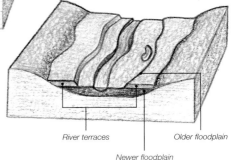

River terraces

Newer floodplain

Older floodplain

Before rejuvenation

New valley

With the help of gravity, the river starts to cut down into the surface below, creating a new valley that is carved into its own flood deposits, leaving terraces on either side.

After rejuvenation

Renewed downcutting

Another way that terraces are created is if the ground is uplifted by tectonic movement, which raises the ground level and causes the river to downcut with renewed erosive power.

New river terraces

River Deltas

As rivers reach a large body of water, such as a sea or a lake, their flow slows, and they branch out into multiple distribution channels, similar to braided rivers (see page 91). These waterways tend to fan out in broad D shapes (hence the name 'delta'), depositing material in gentle slopes. The shape and profile of the deposits depend on the strength of the current from the river and that from the sea or lake, and how these two flows interact.

Delta force

This is an enhanced satellite view of the huge delta of the River Lena in Russia. The delta is approximately 400km (250 miles) wide and extends 100km (62 miles) into the Laptev sea. Vegetation has colonised the sediment deposited by the river and gradually stabilised the ground.

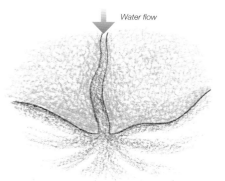

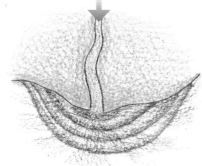

Water flow

Down to the shore

As a river reaches a sea or lake, and its current slows down, the river loses energy and it deposits the sediments it has been carrying at its mouth.

Banking on it

The sediments gradually build up to create new banks of deposits underwater around the river mouth, stretching out from the exit point of the flow.

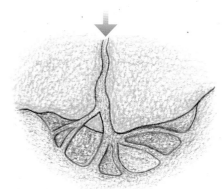

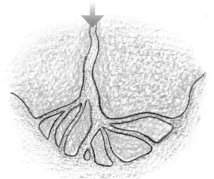

Distribution

The river divides into distributaries, which disperse the energy of the river and its contents. Changes in flow and sediment load change the size and shape of the delta.

New ground

As with the sediments in floodplains, delta deposits are rich in nutrients and plants quickly colonise to benefit from them, creating new ground along the coast.

Freshwater Wetlands

Wetland features in the landscape come in many forms, but they can be broadly divided into freshwater or saltwater wetlands. Naturally, there are degrees of salt levels in the water, depending on the flow and origin of the water, which affect how a wetland develops. Freshwater wetlands, as the name implies, are fed by water from rivers or groundwater, and depend on high groundwater levels. These are characterised by marshy or boggy ground, with waterlogged soil, almost covered by plants.

Flood meadows

River

Sediment

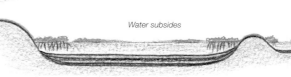

Water subsides

Beginnings of wetlands
Ground becomes saturated by regular flooding or a consistent flow of water from flooding and rainfall. It collects in a man-made or natural hollow, perhaps left by melted ice or an old river channel, creating a shallow lake. The water flow deposits sediment.

Gathering moss
Algae and mosses first colonise the water, building rafts of vegetation that support bacteria and insects. Water-loving plants seed in the nutrient-rich sediment.

Wetland wonderland

Freshwater wetlands, such as this marshland in Doñana National Park in Spain, are highly valued for nature conservation. Sitting on the margins of dry land and water, they provide precious habitats for plants and wildlife.

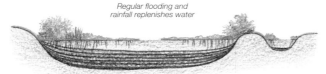

Regular flooding and rainfall replenishes water

Taking root

Small trees and shrubs begin to take root in the colonies of marsh plants and accumulating sediment, their roots binding sediment for other plants to grow on.

Marsh dries out and vegetation grows

Into the woods

Eventually, more small trees and shrubs begin to encroach. They take over the marsh as it dries out and becomes deoxygenised, turning the wetland into woodland or fens.

Fens & Bogs

Fens and bogs are formed over great periods of time and are rich in damp, peaty soils. Fens form in neutral to alkaline water in valleys or hollows. Acid valley bogs tend to occur in sandy or sandstone areas, where flowing water is acidic. Raised bogs are also acidic and form in lowlands from fens or valley bogs when peat gradually accumulates and raises the bog surface above the water level so it is fed only by rainfall. Blanket peat bogs form in uplands in high-rainfall areas.

Peat bog
The peat bog on Creag Choinnich in the Cairngorms, Scotland. The moisture in the bog is very acidic, encouraging plants such as sphagnum moss, which is critical to the formation of peat.

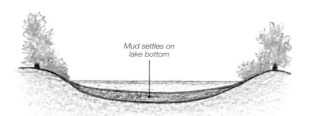

Mud settles on lake bottom

Formation of a fen

Organic material, including dead plants and animals, falls in the lake. As neutral/alkaline water flows in, plants colonise the nutrient-rich soil to form a fen.

Lake

A lake forms in a hollow or indentation in the ground, fed by groundwater and rainfall. Mud collects on the impervious bottom of the lake bed, slowly building up.

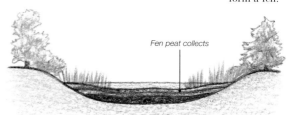

Fen peat collects

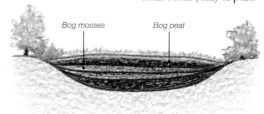

Fen peat fills up lake

Formation of peat

As the bog surface rises above the groundwater, it is fed only by rainwater and so increases in acidity. It can take up to 100 years to form 10cm (4in) of peat.

Formation of a bog

In moist, oxygen-free conditions, the plants do not decompose, but form peat. The peaty sediments fill up the lake, slowly raising the level of the soil above the groundwater.

Bog mosses   Bog peat

Estuaries & Mudflats

Mudflats (right)
The intertidal mudflats of the River Alde in Suffolk, UK, reveal the river channels at low tide. Saltwater-tolerant vegetation is encroaching at the mudflat margins.

Estuaries are the outlets of rivers as they meet the sea, and their shape, width and depth are governed by their origin as well as the river's current, the amount of sediment it carries and the strength of the tide that it meets. Saltwater from the sea and freshwater from the river mix, and the interacting currents cause sand, silt and clay to be deposited. The mudflats that you can see at low tide are the accumulation of these deposits. Estuaries can be formed in several different ways.

Rift valley
River estuaries were also occasionally created by tectonic movement opening up a rift, causing the ground to drop, allowing an inflow of seawater.

Drowned rivers
Most estuaries were created when sea levels rose at the end of the last ice age, effectively 'drowning' well-established river valleys leading down to the sea.

Sediment builds up in bottom of estuary

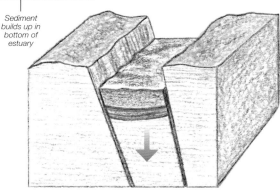

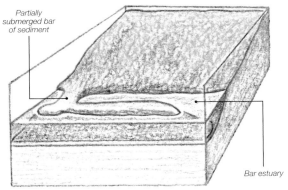

Partially submerged bar of sediment

Bar estuary

Up to the bar

A bar-built estuary is formed when bars of sand and gravel are deposited along a shoreline (see page 178), trapping the estuary parallel to the coast.

Saltwater Marshes

Coastal marsh (right)
This saltmarsh on Mellum island in the German North Sea is turning green as plants colonise it. These coastal areas are a rich habitat for wildlife and specialised plants.

When the river reaches the sea, the channels in estuaries often become more and more silted up by deposits from the river itself or the rising and falling tides of the sea. This means that the resulting mudflats become exposed to the air, and not covered by saltwater, for longer and longer periods. As this happens, a range of plants adapted to the salty environment begin to move in and colonise the mudflats, benefiting from the nutrient-rich mud. In tropical regions, mangrove trees colonise such swamps.

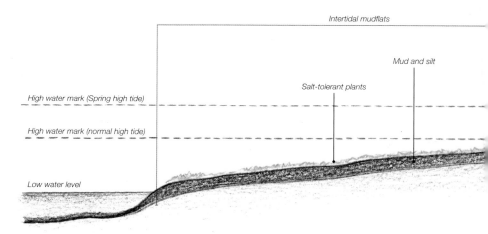

Intertidal mudflats

Mud and silt

Salt-tolerant plants

High water mark (Spring high tide)

High water mark (normal high tide)

Low water level

Intertidal mudflats
As in freshwater marshes, the accumulation of sediments on estuarine mudflats leads to opportunistic plants moving in and colonising the exposed mud.

Colonisation
However, the tidal and saltwater nature of the habitat attracts plants that tolerate submersion in saltwater for up to eight hours during the twelve-hour tidal cycle.

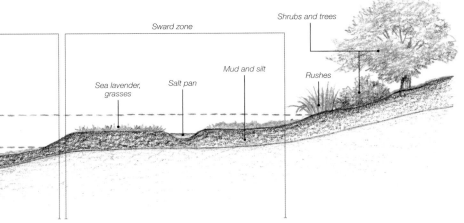

Shrubs and trees

Sward zone

Mud and silt

Sea lavender,
grasses

Salt pan

Rushes

Live by the sward

Parts of the marsh, known as the sward zone, are submerged only during the highest tides each month. The plants in this area, such as sea lavender, can only tolerate being submerged for four hours in twelve.

Salt pans

Channels allow water to enter and leave the marsh, but hollows, or salt pans, form where saltwater becomes trapped between the vegetation at low tide. When the water evaporates, it leaves salt levels on the mud.

Saltflats

Saltflats are found in mainly dry or arid regions. They are actually a particular form of dry lake bed, known as a playa or pan. Playas are formed by occasional rain, or a rising water table, filling low-lying areas of flat ground. The water then evaporates to leave behind the dried sediment and, in the case of saltflats, mud with a high concentration of salt.

Salt of the earth
Bonneville Saltflats in Utah, USA. The polygonal cracking seen on the surface of the ground happens on many dried mud playas when the mud shrinks as the moisture content evaporates. Regular flooding and evaporation of the flats creates a smooth surface.

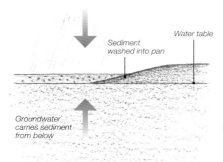

Temporary lake

Water from rainfall or a rising water table fills a wide, flat plain in an arid climate, collecting in a wide, shallow indentation in the ground to form a temporary lake.

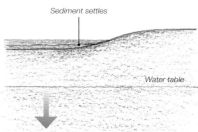

Lake dries

During a prolonged period without any further rainfall, the flow of groundwater subsides and the lake gradually dries up, water evaporating in the heat.

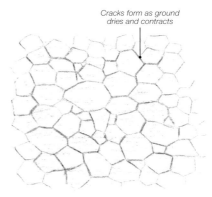

Residual minerals

The water evaporates to leave behind sediments such as mud, sand or silt, as well as minerals such as salts, in high concentrations on the surface.

Snap and crackle

The mud-and-salt mixture shrinks as it dries, often forming polygonal surface cracks. The salt crystallises in the cracks, wedging them open.

Lakes

Lakes vary widely in size and in origin. Many lakes are formed when water flowing from rivers, rainwater or groundwater collects in a large depression in the ground, but usually several processes are involved in creating lakes. Water from these sources may become blocked by changes in the land. Also, glaciation can create depressions in the ground. The diagrams illustrate a few of the many ways a lake can be formed over time. Lakes tend to be short-lived features, geologically speaking, as other processes, such as deposition of sediment, evaporation of water, or erosion of lakesides, may ultimately drain them.

Great Lakes
The Great Lakes on the Canada-USA border sit in valleys that were originally opened up by plate movement. The valleys were then deepened further by glacial action, and when the glaciers retreated, the meltwaters filled the basins.

Volcanic lakes

We have seen how lakes form in the calderas of extinct or dormant volcanoes (page 65). Lava flows can also dam the flow of a river to create a lake.

Landslides

Slope failure on valley sides can cause earth and rock to fall down hillsides and block rivers, creating a new lake behind the natural dam.

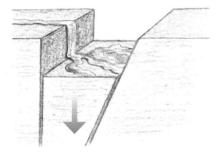

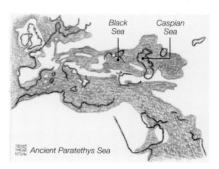

Ancient Paratethys Sea

Lakes created by tectonic movement

Depressions can be created by the movement of tectonic plates, by folding or down-warping of the ground, for instance, or when rift valleys are created by faults.

Enclosure of a sea

A sea may become landlocked when sea levels fall. The Black and Caspian seas were isolated as the result of tectonic uplift and falling sea levels about five mya.

COASTS

Introduction

Making the coast (right)
Coasts tend to change rapidly because they are exposed to deposition and erosion by wind and water, and to chemical and mechanical breakdown.

In the previous section we read how rivers begin to deposit their loads, for instance, in flats and deltas, when they slow down on reaching the larger mass of water in the sea. While rivers deposit sediment at their mouths, the sea also deposits sand along the shore. Erosion, caused by the action of wind and waves on the sea, also acts on the features on the shore. As with other landscapes, these two opposing forces of erosion and deposition work together on an area's underlying rock to shape each coastline.

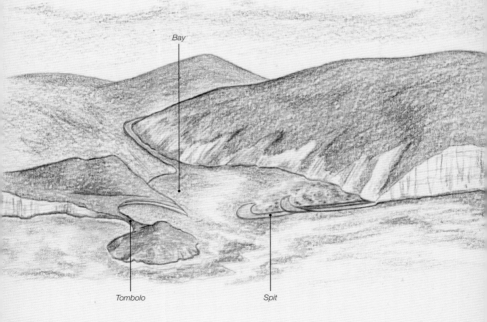

Bay

Tombolo

Spit

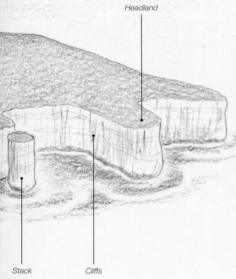

Headland

Stack

Cliffs

Time and tides

We've seen how land is created by tectonic activity, forging new ground from deep in the crust, raising the ground during the collision of plates, and then breaking down and eroding over time. Where the land comes into contact with the sea, it is subject to constant forces of deposition, transportation and erosion, carrying, building up and wearing down rock and deposits. The sea is moved in waves by wind on its surface, and by tidal forces generated by the gravitational pull of the Moon and the Sun and the rotation of the Earth. The tides and wind also generate local currents, which throw the waves at the shore, pulverising rock into finer particles and then using these particles to erode the rock still further. The tides and currents also deposit or remove particles on the shore, depending on the combination of forces, tides and rock types.

Cliffs

Cliff face

These cliffs at Hunstanton on the north Norfolk coast, UK, are constantly crumbling in the face of the continued onslaught from powerful waves.

The tall sea cliffs that we see along many parts of our coasts are among the most obvious features created by erosion in our landscape. Uplifted above sea level by such forces as plate movement or the rebalancing of the landmasses when heavy ice melted, the exposed rock is subject to huge natural forces. Crumbling and retreating in the face of the onslaught of the sea, cliffs are created by the constant pressures of several processes of erosion.

Shockwaves

The waves are thrown against the landmass by winds and currents. Tall waves contain a great deal of energy, which transmit large shockwaves through the ground on impact, shaking it and weakening rock structurally.

Landslides

If the ground consists of soft rock strata, such as silt, clay or limestones, the shock from waves or the saturation by seawater and heavy rain can cause the ground to collapse, creating land- or rockslides.

Corrosion and solution

The salt and carbonic acid in the seawater dissolves the particles in some rock types, such as limestones. Salt particles also create crystals as they evaporate, expanding as they form to break apart cracks in the rock.

Abrasion

As rock crumbles from the cliff face, the smaller rock materials join the sand, shingle and boulders already in the seawater, and are thrown against the rock, breaking up its surface still further.

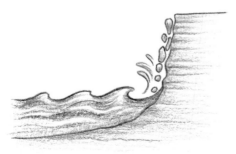

Caves

Sea cave
This cave in cliffs along the Portuguese coast has not fallen in yet because of the strength of the surrounding rock layers. It's only a matter of time, however.

The previous two pages showed how the sea attacks the edge of a landmass to create cliff faces. Some of these cliffs also feature caves. These cavities, which tunnel back into the base of a cliff, are created by the same processes of erosion that relentlessly abrade or corrode away the rock at specific points of weakness in the cliff face. Some caves may be found higher up a cliff and this indicates that the cave was eroded many years before, when the sea level was at the same height as the cave.

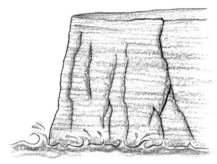

Cracks

Constant battering by waves exploits vertical lines of weakness in the cliffs, such as cracks, joints or faults that are formed as the result of stresses in the rock.

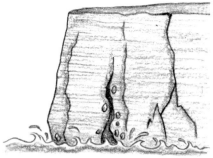

Rock breakdown

The force of waves is strongest at the base of a cliff where erosion gradually widens the lines of weakness, opening the cavities into larger holes in the cliff.

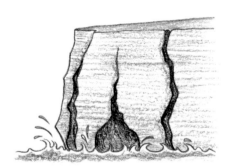

Cave

A cave is gradually opened up in the cliff. If the rock is resistant enough, it will hold its shape around the cave. It will be some time before erosion and rock breakdown cause the cave to collapse.

Blowholes

Sometimes erosion creates a narrow vertical crevice which concentrates the force of the waves. The waves push a column of air up through the crevice, which forces open a shaft or blowhole.

Shore Platform

Platform game

This shore platform on the Glamorgan coast in South Wales is what remains after the cliffs have been eroded away by the waves. The platform extends out some distance into the sea.

Often found at the base of a stretch of rocky cliffs, a flat, or more correctly, a very gently sloping platform of rock stretches out for a short distance into the sea. This platform has been created by the retreat of the cliffs, and has subsequently been further corroded or eroded by material washed against its surface during tidal movements. Since the waves are forced to travel further across the platform as the cliff face retreats, dissipating their energy, the platform has the effect of reducing the erosion of the cliffs over time.

Cliff attack

As the waves pound against the rock at sea level and above, they begin to corrode or abrade the cliff, gradually eroding the rock, causing it to crumble and collapse.

Rock fall

As the rock is weakened by waves and salt attack, the cliff begins to crack and disintegrate. The rock fragments fall onto the newly cut platform below.

Platform

The force of the sea, particularly during storms, breaks up and washes away the cliff fragments that have fallen from its face, to reveal the newly created flat bench of rock, the shore platform, at low tide. The shore platform stretches out at a shallow angle from the bottom of the cliff gradually inclining down into the sea.

Bays & Coves

Many coastlines consist of a series of headlands and bays. Bays and the distinctive, rounded forms called coves, are natural harbours that form when the erosive forces of the sea find and exploit weaknesses in the rock of a coastline. These weaknesses take the form of areas of less resistant rock that is broken up and worn away more quickly. Twin headlands form either side and the force of the waves becomes concentrated on the headlands instead.

Lulworth Cove
Circular bays are known as coves, one of the most remarkable being Lulworth Cove in Dorset, UK. The sea has broken through a gap in the wall of resistant Portland stone, and worn away a circular bay in the softer band of clay behind.

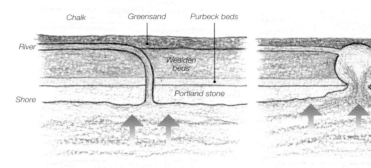

Soft rock

As waves impact on a shore, the various processes of erosion, including corrosion and abrasion, take effect on an exposed area of less resistant rock.

Wash-out

Rock is broken away and waves rush into the newly created bay during high tides and storms, washing out loose rocks and exposing more of the softer material.

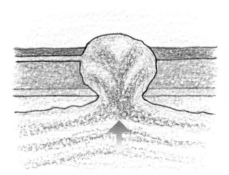

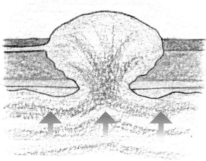

Back of the bay

As the bay is opened out, the force of the waves is gradually dissipated. This causes erosion to reduce, and deposits of sand and shingle to build up in the bay.

Going sideways

The strength of the waves is redirected onto the sides of the headland. A cove is formed when the headlands deflect the waves so that they carve out a circular bay.

Headlands

Headlands mostly consist of resistant rock that juts out into the sea between areas of softer rock or natural weaknesses in the ground. Although the force of the waves is initially focused on the less resistant rock in between, opening up bays and coves (see pages 168–169), the main force of erosion is gradually transferred to the exposed finger of rock, which it breaks down and wears it away over time until it disappears entirely.

Old headland
The famous Old Harry Rocks at Studland, Dorset, UK, are what remains of the old chalk headland. They will eventually be washed away by the sea. You can still see the shallow platform that was the base of the cliffs beneath the surface of the blue water.

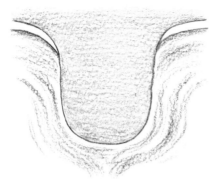

Wave force

We have seen how a bay is gradually opened up by erosion. and as the strength of the waves is dissipated beaches of sand and shingle are built up.

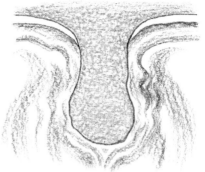

Exposed

The exposed headland is now attacked by the encircling waves. which are thrown against the sides of the headland by its shape. This accelerates the erosion rate.

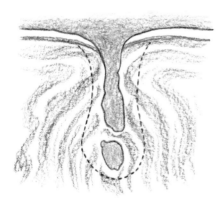

Narrow

Erosion ruthlessly exploits weaknesses in the headland walls to create caves (page 164) and arches and stacks (page 172), thereby narrowing it.

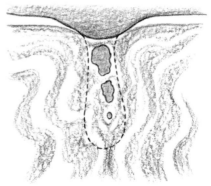

Breaking up

The stacks are broken apart by erosion. which attacks weaknesses in the rock. so that all that is left of the headland is an area of rocky shallows below sea level.

Arches & Stacks

Stack and arch
The stack and arch at Etretat, in Normandy, France, made famous by Impressionist painters. They are the remnants of a headland that once stretched out into the English Channel.

The jagged rocks that perch at the end of headlands are further, impressive evidence of the erosive power of the sea as well as being a demonstration of the process of marine erosion. Tall towers of rock, called stacks, are sometimes accompanied by great arches. These forms both stand as relics of a once-prominent headland, marking its position stretching out into the sea. The waves encircle a headland, constantly attacking it from both sides until they reduce it to the ruins that we see today.

Headland

As explained on pages 170–171, the erosive action of the waves gradually reduces a headland of resistant rock to a narrow promontory that juts out into the sea.

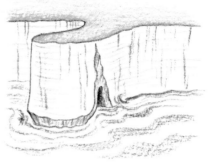

Arching out

As the waves continue to attack either side of the cliff face, they form caves in the base of the rock. Eventually, the caves meet, creating a tunnel through the headland.

Stacking up

The rock reaches a point when it is no longer able to support the weight of the arch roof, causing the arch to collapse and creating an isolated tower of rock.

Falling tower

The rock tower is then worn away at its base and sides by the action of the waves, and from the top by rain and frost, so that it gradually collapses into the sea.

Beaches & Dunes

Life's a beach
A beach acts as a buffer zone between the dry land and the sea. In many cases, except at very low tides, you will see only a small proportion of it above the waves.

So far we have looked at coastal features caused by erosion – the removal of material. However, many of us are perhaps most familiar with beaches. A beach is a depositional feature that forms when the force of the waves is reduced in shallower depths, causing the waves to deposit more sand, gravel and shingle than they are able to carry away. The shape of a beach therefore depends on the direction and strength of the approaching waves and the size of sediment being deposited on the shore.

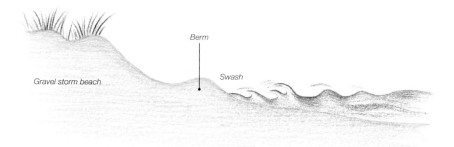

Gravel storm beach

Berm

Swash

Deposition of sediments

Waves that move more backwards and forwards and less up and down are 'constructive' and deposit more material than they can carry away. 'Destructive' waves are tall and carry more material away from the beach. Gravel or shingle beaches are steeper than sandy beaches because water washes down through the coarse particles more easily, carrying fewer particles back down the beach. Storm beaches are the highest part of a shingle beach, where high tides have carried the largest material.

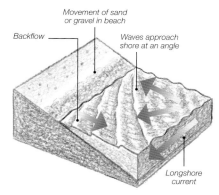

Movement of sand or gravel in beach

Backflow

Waves approach shore at an angle

Longshore current

Wave-formed

As waves approach a beach at an angle, they slow in the shallower water, rising and bunching together. They flow up the beach in a forward 'swash' movement, carrying sediment onto the beach at an angle, and then falling back with reduced energy.

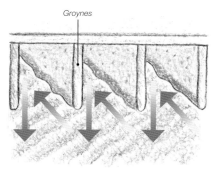

Groynes

Longshore drift

This motion causes sand and gravel particles to be picked up and deposited along the shoreline. Groynes are often erected on sandy beaches that are important for tourism, to prevent material being washed away from the beach.

Spits

Like beaches, spits are features of deposition that occur when the amounts of sand and shingle being moved by the sea exceed the ability of the waves to carry the material away. Spits comprise long, narrow bars of sand, shingle, or both, that stretch out from the mainland, usually extending into a bay or estuary mouth. Where the spits become stable and protect large areas of shallow, intertidal water, sediment gets deposited behind them and a saltmarsh (see page 154) often forms.

Blakeney Point
This view of the shingle spit of Blakeney Point on the northern Norfolk coast, UK, clearly shows its development. Each hook of shingle and sand has been caused by prolonged strong winds and waves pushing material back into the bay. Vegetation has begun to populate and stabilise the older and more stable banks of the spit.

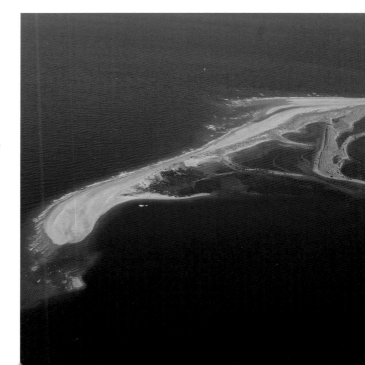

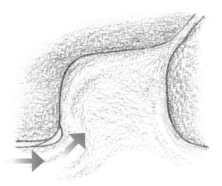

Spit starts

A spit begins to form when longshore drift carries pebbles, gravel and sand past the old headland, depositing it where the water shallows and slows.

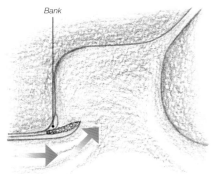

Bank

Storm force

During storms or very high tides, large quantities of the larger pebbles and shingle are thrown high up to form a more durable bank of material.

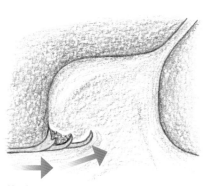

Hooks

The spit grows with time, developing hook-like ends when deflected waves, during high tides and storms, deposit shingle and pebbles further into the bay.

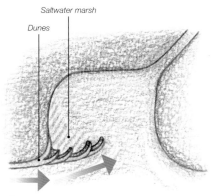

Saltwater marsh

Dunes

Dunes

At low tide, dried-out sand grains from the beach may be lifted by the wind and deposited further inland to form dunes. Vegetation grows and stabilises the spit.

Bars & Tombolos

On Chesil beach

The long stretch of Chesil beach – a barrier beach – has built up to form a type of tombolo joining the Isle of Portland to the English mainland in Dorset, UK.

Bars are beaches that form when sand or shingle is deposited between two headlands across a bay. Bars create natural banks that protect the water they enclose from tidal waters, sometimes enclosing a bay altogether to create a lagoon. Like all beaches they are subject to the force of the waves, accumulating sediment during quiet weather and losing it during heavy storms, which may breach the bars. Tombolos are types of bar that connect islands or an island and the mainland together.

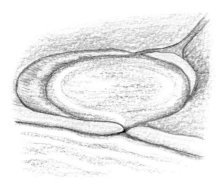

Bay watch

Drift carrying sand and shingle along the coast may deposit material across the opening of a bay, connecting the two sides together to create a baymouth bar.

Called to the bar

Like a spit, a bar of sand or shingle builds up when material is deposited by slowing currents. Bars are often deposited parallel to the coast by longshore drift.

Tombolos

A tombolo forms where the currents slow between two outcrops of land, for instance between the mainland and an island, allowing a bank of sand or shingle to build up between them, joining them together.

Barrier islands

Where the offshore underwater topography is very shallow, a sand bar may build up parallel to the coast, creating a strip of barrier islands, as on the eastern and Gulf coasts of the USA.

Reefs

Coastal reef

The Great Barrier Reef off the coast of Queensland in northeast Australia is the world's largest reef system. It consists of more than 2,900 separate coral reefs.

Coral reefs are coastal features that are found in shallow, warm-water seas. They consist of limestone built up from many layers of the hard parts, such as the shells, of water-dwelling organisms and the secretions of corals. The reefs provide a valuable habitat for many living organisms, including algae that support each other and add to the reef when they die and decay. Reefs can form along a shoreline or parallel to a coast, separated from it by a large lagoon. The largest reef is the Great Barrier Reef off the coast of Australia. Islands called atolls are also reef structures.

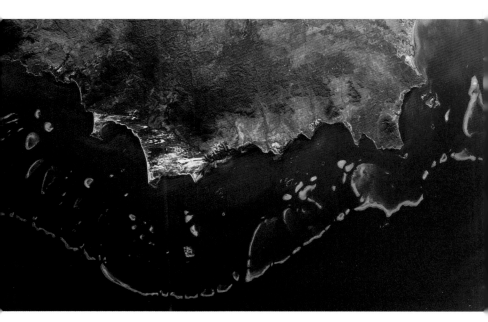

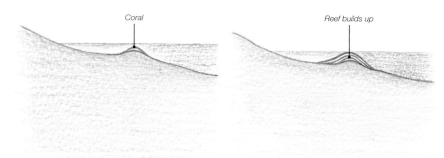

Reef build-up

A coral colony begins when a free-swimming animal, a coral polyp, attaches itself to an underwater rock along the edge of an island or coastline. The polyp reproduces asexually, giving rise to a colony of corals that gradually expands outwards, building up a reef that attracts other creatures. The most common type of reef, a fringing reef, forms against a shoreline, and slowly builds up away from the shore.

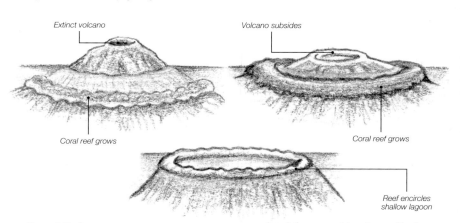

How atolls form

Atolls are circular ring islands made from coral with a central lagoon. The biologist Charles Darwin was the first to put forward a theory to explain them, which is still considered basically valid today. He speculated that a coral barrier reef built up around a volcano. Over time, the volcano subsided – or the sea level rose, or both – leaving a ring-like reef, encircling a shallow lagoon with a floor made from the old coral.

Effects of Changing Sea Level

Raised coastline
McWay Falls, on the Big Sur Coast in California, USA. The waterfall cascades from a V-shaped hanging valley high above sea level; this shows that the land has risen above sea level more quickly than the river has been able to erode it.

Coastlines are affected by huge forces. The movement of plates can raise landmasses and ice ages can generate massive ice sheets that absorb large quantities of seawater, lowering sea levels around the globe. Also, prolonged periods of rising temperatures can melt the ice sheets, causing sea levels to rise, but also reducing the weight of the overlying ice sheets, causing the ground to rise up again. All of these changes affect the coastal landscape. Many emergent coastlines are characterised by rocky cliffs, with ancient beaches on top of the cliffs.

Submerged coasts

On earlier pages we saw how estuaries, rias and fjords are formed by the rising of sea level, or the falling of the landmass, or both. These coastal landforms are known as submergent or drowned coasts. Hilly landscapes that become submerged turn into a group of islands, with the tops of the hills standing above water level.

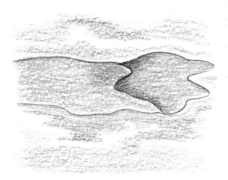

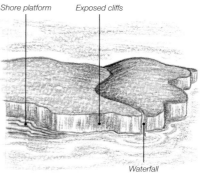

Shore platform Exposed cliffs

Waterfall

Emergent coasts

Rising or emergent coastlines, such as the Pacific coast of the USA, occur when sea level falls and/or the land is raised by tectonic uplift, for instance. These coasts often include several shore platforms (page 166) that look like broad steps, demonstrating how the sea level has occupied higher levels in the past.

KARST Introduction

Karst landscape
Soil and vegetation contribute to the carbonic acid content of the water that flows over and through limestone rocks. The flow of rock fragments in acidic water aids the erosive action.

Until now, we have tended to look at various landforms or features that are broadly characteristic of landscapes depending on their geographical position rather than rock composition. However, it is worth focusing specifically on what are called karst landscapes. These develop in areas where the underlying rock is permeable, such as limestone, and is subject to erosion by large amounts of rain and groundwater. These circumstances give rise to recognisable features that are particular to this type of landscape.

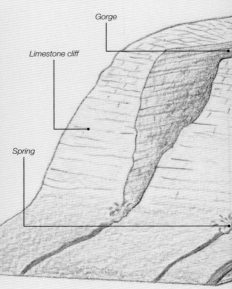

Gorge

Limestone cliff

Spring

Spring

Dissolved world

Rocks such as limestone, which are made from millions of tiny shells and the skeletons of sea creatures, are hard but permeable, because of the gaps and cracks that are present throughout their layers. These rocks are also soluble and susceptible to chemical breakdown. Rain and groundwater carry high levels of carbonic acid and as rain falls on the rocks, the acid dissolves limestone and the water carries it away in solution as it drains down through the rock. The result is that these landscapes display signs of this erosive action in characteristic geological features, including holes in the ground, dry valleys, gorges, caves and limestone pavements.

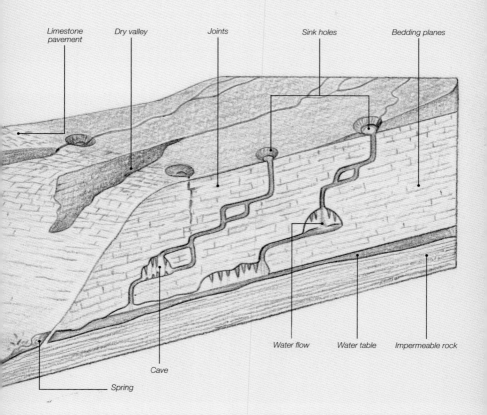

Limestone pavement

Dry valley

Joints

Sink holes

Bedding planes

Water flow

Water table

Impermeable rock

Cave

Spring

Karst Landscape Evolution

Karst towers
Abundant rain, together with large amounts of vegetation, can erode large areas, leaving prominent cones or towers behind as seen here at Yangshuo, in Guangxi province in China.

Karst landscapes develop over many years as rainwater gradually dissolves and erodes the layers of a limestone-dominated landscape by exploiting cracks and joints. Over time, the landscape is reshaped, reducing it to the lower, more resistant layers of rock underneath the limestone. The cycle of development of a karst landscape is often thought of as being divided into four phases: formation of sinkholes, widening of hollows, followed by erosion into peaks and valleys, and then flat plains.

Sinkholes

Holes develop in the ground (see page 190 on sinkholes), as water finds cracks and joints in the rock, gradually dissolving it, and soaking deep into the ground.

Large hollows

Over time, the water dissolves the rock to widen the holes into much larger hollows, known as 'cockpits', which begin to merge into one another.

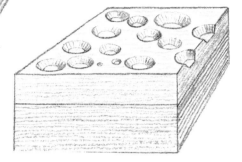

Peaks and valleys

Gradually, the hillsides are eroded away to create areas of low-lying, flat terrain, and smaller, isolated peaks stretching above it.

Open plains

The ground is slowly levelled out by water erosion, leaving wide plains with isolated peaks, the remnants of the higher ground.

Potholes, Caves & Caverns

Running water is the main cause of the erosion and weathering of limestone, both above and below ground. We have seen how water ruthlessly exploits weaknesses in the landscape to gradually wear a route downhill that allows it to flow to lower ground as quickly as possible. The same happens where the rock is unable to resist it, such as in limestone and karst landscapes. Here the water flows down cracks and joints in the limestone, gradually dissolving the rock and creating large holes.

Karst spring
This spring is the source of the River Loue and emerges from a cave at the foot of a limestone cliff located in the Jura mountains in France.

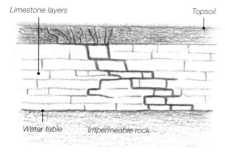

Limestone layers — Topsoil

Water table — Impermeable rock

Flowing underground

Where rivers or groundwater reach areas of limestone rock, the water quickly finds the cracks and joints between the rock, and flows along the bedding planes, where it dissolves the rock and erodes it.

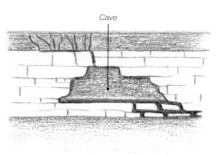

Cave

Potholes and caves

The acidic water widens the cracks into potholes and underground channels. Where the water collects in underground pools, particularly during floods, it dissolves and erodes the rock to create caverns and caves.

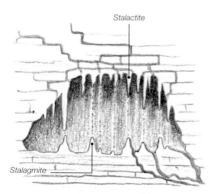

Stalactite

Stalagmite

Stalactites and stalagmites

The carbonic acid in the water reacts with the calcium carbonate in the limestone. When this solution drips into open caves, the carbon dioxide is lost to the air, and the evaporating solution forms crystals. These crystals form stalactites and stalagmites.

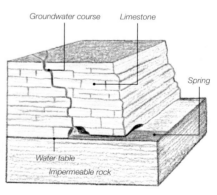

Groundwater course — Limestone

Spring

Water table

Impermeable rock

Spring

When the groundwater reaches an impermeable layer of rock beneath the limestone, it flows along the layer until it finds its way to the surface, usually at the junction between the limestone and the impermeable rock layers.

Sinkholes

Sinkholes are rounded holes that appear in the ground in limestone or karst landscapes. Also known as dolines, sinkholes can appear individually, or in large groups. In 'young' karst landscapes, large numbers of dolines indicate that the ground will eventually be eroded away. There are two basic kinds of these holes that you may encounter – sinkholes created by a process of water dissolving the rock in a weak spot, or collapsed sinkholes. Some sinkholes become filled with debris through which the water cannot permeate, and so small lakes form in them.

Sinkhole
This sinkhole shows how water dissolves and undermines limestone. These indentations in the ground tend to be common in areas with underlying limestone and show where the water is gradually dissolving the rock below.

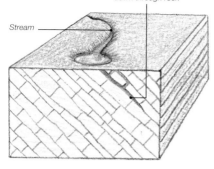

Down the cracks

Water runs over or through the ground until it comes to layers of limestone. If the layers lie at an angle, water can attack the joints and cracks between bedding planes.

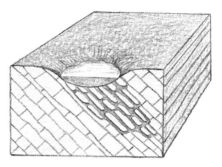

Indentation

The water gradually dissolves and carries away the limestone down through the ground, creating an indentation on the surface which collects more water.

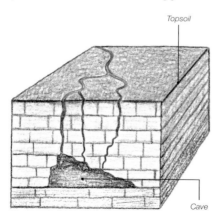

Underground cavities

As groundwater percolates down through the upper layers of soil and rock, it dissolves and widens cracks in the limestone, creating underground cavities.

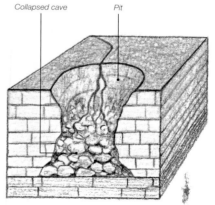

Collapse

The soil and rock above is gradually washed away until it reaches a point at which the ground suddenly gives way, collapsing into an underground cave below.

Limestone Arches

KARST

Limestone arch
The Pont d'Arc limestone bridge in the Ardèche region of southern France. A popular tourist attraction, the arch will eventually collapse when the eroded rock can no longer support its own weight.

Another feature of limestone landscapes is the natural arch. These come in a range of shapes and sizes, but they are all essentially the remnants of tunnels that were eroded by the flow of water through the rock. They are a later development of the caves or caverns that we read about on pages 188–189. They often mark the spot where an underground stream originally emerged between the layer of limestone and a lower impermeable layer of rock, through the base of a cliff.

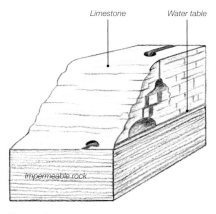

Limestone   Water table

Impermeable rock

Excavation

As we have already seen, water flows underground in limestone rock formations to create subterranean channels and caves by dissolution and erosion.

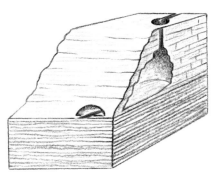

Cavernous

During times of flood, large volumes of water fill the caverns, dissolving the rock and carrying fragments away, speeding up the process of erosion.

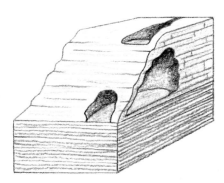

End of the tunnel

The underground caves are enlarged as the water flow dissolves and erodes the rock, until there is no longer enough material to support the cave roofs and they collapse.

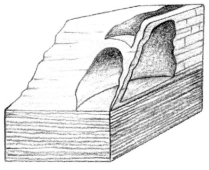

Arch

Rock arches are what remain of the ancient underground tunnels, until they also become too weak to support themselves and in due course collapse as well.

Limestone Pavements

Some exposed areas of limestone, with their long cracks and mosaics of flat-topped stones, resemble man-made pavements. The layer of limestone has been exposed to rain by the removal of the soil covering, for instance, by glaciation. The rain has then exploited the joints and cracks in the limestone, dissolving the rock along the cracks to create the network of channels.

Crazy paving

The famous limestone pavement in Yorkshire, UK. The cracks, or grikes, between the rocks are slowly being widened and you can see from the texture of the blocks of limestone how the rain is weathering them. The cracks provide a habitat for rare, specialist plants.

Layer exposed

The limestone is scraped clear of soil and exposed to the elements when a glacier melts. Water seeps down the cracks and joints in the rock.

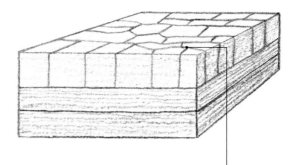

Exposed top limestone layer

Dissolution

The carbonic acid in the water reacts with the alkaline limestone, dissolving it into fine particles, which running water washes away along the cracks or down into the rock.

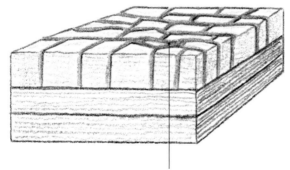

Running water

Cracks in time

Over time, the chemical action of the water widens the cracks (known as grikes), while rain weathers the raised blocks of limestone (called clints), so lowering them.

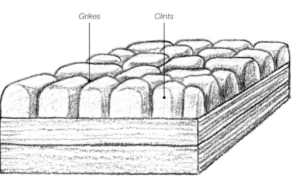

Grikes *Clints*

Introduction

There is a wide range of landscapes found across different regions of the Earth, all of varied types of rock and tectonic activity. Some of these regions have certain climatic conditions in common, however, that affect the landscapes you find there: tropical, desert, periglacial and geothermal. These types of landscape are covered in the following pages. Tropical regions, for example, share high average temperatures and frequent and heavy rainfall. Many landforms around the world were once formed in tropical regions and have since migrated to other climates as the planet's tectonic plates have moved.

Totally tropical
The best-known tropical areas are the Amazon Basin in South America and the Congo Basin in central Africa. Other areas include Malaysia, Indonesia and southern Vietnam. It is believed that the high humidity and rainfall in some tropical areas account for many low-relief plains, which have been heavily eroded and coated in large amounts of sediment by rivers.

Tropical seas

Some limestone rock formations in Britain demonstrate the abundance of sea life, including corals, in ancient tropical seas, before the organisms were fossilised in many layers of sediment on the sea bed.

Swamps

Large areas of wetlands form in tropical conditions, including mangrove swamps. The roots allow silts to build up in layers with organic deposits, over time forming coal and gas beds deep beneath the ground.

Peaks

The heavy rainfall in the tropics results in the extreme breakdown and erosion that we see in karst landscapes (see page 184). Here the additional biological activity raises water acidity, aiding rock breakdown.

Plains and inselbergs

Extreme and long-term erosion and sediment deposition lead to flat landscapes or peneplains (see page 135), particularly in tectonically stable areas. Residual hills or outcrops, called inselbergs, may remain.

Desert Landscapes

The common view of deserts as areas of windswept sand dunes is not accurate. As with tropical regions, desert landscapes vary widely, and can include 'cold deserts' at high altitudes, where temperatures in winter drop well below zero, stony or rocky deserts, and semi-arid deserts, where there is enough moisture to sustain limited vegetation. What these areas all have in common is the lack of regular rainfall. This means that the dry ground and rock are exposed to forms of breakdown and erosion characteristic of deserts.

Onion rocks

These bizarre onion-like rocks in the Bisti Badlands, New Mexico, USA, exhibit signs of wind erosion, which has rounded out their bases, as well as rock breakdown. The 'exfoliated' rocks have been attacked by a combination of moisture and salt infiltrating their surfaces, which have expanded in the sun and contracted in the cold, breaking them apart in layers.

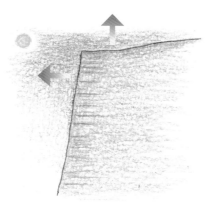

Rock breakdown

In desert conditions, under often cloudless skies, the rock surface is exposed to extremes of temperature. During the day, the Sun heats up the rock face, which then expands.

Cracks

At night, temperatures can drop to well below zero, especially in winter. As a result of the expansion and contraction, cracks form in the rock surface.

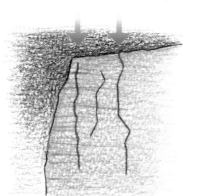

Dew

Rapid loss of temperature at night causes dew to form, and this seeps into cracks in the rock face and reacts chemically with it, as well as freezing and thawing.

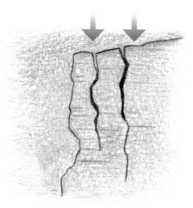

Salt attack

Salts in solution in the moisture can also attack the rock surface. As the water evaporates, the salt forms crystals that expand and break open surface cracks.

Wind Erosion & Deposition

Without regular or substantial rainfall, many desert areas are subjected to erosion by dry sand and rock particles being carried by the wind and abrading rock surfaces, gradually eroding them. Fine sand particles are lifted by winds and carried great distances. Larger, coarser particles are lifted short distances by strong winds or pushed along by large amounts of the wind-blown fine sand particles. These particle movements cause several kinds of erosional and depositional land features in deserts.

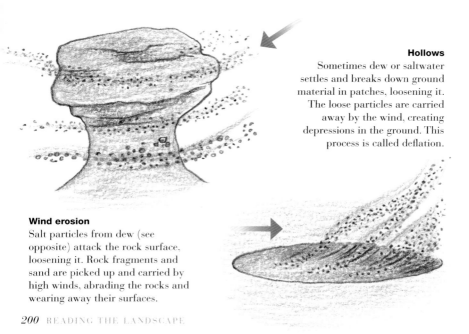

Hollows
Sometimes dew or saltwater settles and breaks down ground material in patches, loosening it. The loose particles are carried away by the wind, creating depressions in the ground. This process is called deflation.

Wind erosion
Salt particles from dew (see opposite) attack the rock surface, loosening it. Rock fragments and sand are picked up and carried by high winds, abrading the rocks and wearing away their surfaces.

Crescent dunes

Curving seif or linear sand dunes in the Namib desert, in Namibia, reveal how fine sand grains can be deposited by desert winds. The ripples show how the sand is moved up the slope of the dune by wind blowing from the left of the picture and carried over the sheer edge.

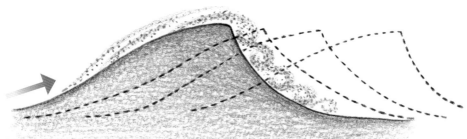

Dunes

As wind speeds slow, so the sand grains fall to the ground in piles. The sand accumulates and forms dunes across large areas, sometimes of hundreds or thousands of square kilometres/miles. The shapes of the dunes, which often form around rocks or objects on the ground, are decided by wind speed and direction, as well as other factors including the amount of sand and vegetation and the type of ground. Continuing winds constantly reshape and move the dunes.

Water Erosion & Deposition

As we have already established, rainfall in deserts is rare and unpredictable. However, it has occurred in the past and still does occur, often in sudden downpours, which affect the shape of the landscape. Many deserts contain wadis, steep-sided ravines created by large, fast-flowing rivers caused by flash floods. Without vegetation, the water washes away large quantities of already heavily weathered and eroded rock fragments, breaking them up further and depositing them across plains, or playas.

Wet wadi
A wadi or gully in the desert in Morocco runs with water. The ravine was cut by the river in times of flood in the past.

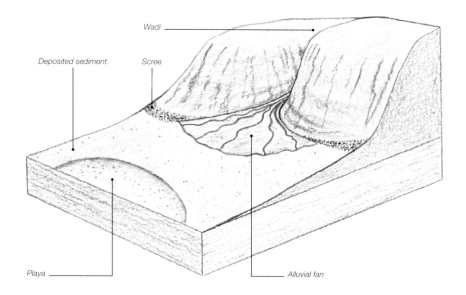

Wadi

Deposited sediment

Scree

Playa

Alluvial fan

Wadis, pediments and playas

Water does flow in rivers in some deserts, either because the river originates outside the desert region or because it drains into an inland lake. Mostly, however, rivers flow only intermittently or seasonally as the result of severe rainstorms. The water is unable to soak into the parched ground because the surface has become impermeable. Also only sparse vegetation exists to soak up or deflect the flow of water. If it falls in large enough quantities on relatively flat surfaces, the rain generates sheet floods that carry and deposit sand and gravel on the desert floor in large carpets. However, where the water can exploit cracks in the rock, it quickly

creates steep-sided ravines called wadis. These are dry most of the time but are subject to occasional, unpredictable flash floods, although it is thought that wadis originally formed during times of more frequent and heavier rainfall. At the base of higher ground, and where wadis open out, an alluvial fan (see page 100) is usually found spreading out onto a pediment, a gentle rock-cut slope often covered with deposits of sediment. Beyond the pediment is a flat plain that can become flooded during occasional rainstorms. The water evaporates to leave behind a desiccated and cracked crust of silt, clay or salt, called a playa.

Periglacial Landscapes

Periglacial polygons (right)
This type of stone patterning is typical of permafrost surfaces in Iceland. The stones have been brought to the surface by frost-heave and have fallen down the raised mounds to form stone lines.

Periglacial landscapes occur in areas where the ground surface is frozen solid for much of the time. Today, these areas exist in areas of high latitude, mostly in northern parts of Canada, Alaska, Russia, Greenland and Norway. Here the mean annual temperature is below −5°C (23°F), with summers being very short and intense. These conditions lead to particular kinds of feature in the landscape, some of which may still be found in areas that were once subject to similar conditions during past ice ages.

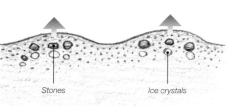
Stones   Ice crystals

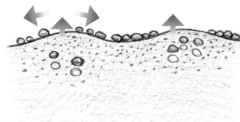

Frost-heave
When ground is subjected to very low temperatures, a phenomenon known as frost-heave occurs, which involves several processes. As fine soils become frozen, they expand, creating small domes in the ground. At the same time, stones in the soil conduct the cold temperature more easily than the surrounding soil, and so pockets of ice crystals form underneath

them, expanding and pushing the stones to the surface. When the temperature rises and the soil thaws, fine material flows under the stones, stopping them from falling back underground. Repeated freezing and thawing sorts the stones so that the heavier ones gradually move outwards to the edges of the domes of soil, thereby creating patterns of polygons or stripes on the surface.

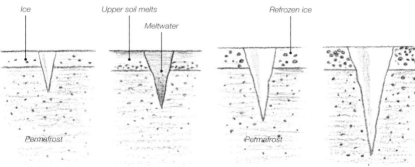

Ice   Upper soil melts   Refrozen ice

Meltwater

Permafrost   Permafrost

Winter to summer

The formation of ice wedges in the ground can also create polygonal patterns. When coarser soils are frozen, they contract, causing cracks to open in the ground. When the ground thaws during the summer, these cracks fill with water and fine sediment.

Subsequent years

The water then freezes again the following winter, causing the cracks to widen. Over time, the ice wedges that form in the cracks become larger. As the region warms and the ice melts, the cracks in the ground fill up with silt creating casts of the ice wedges.

Periglacial Features

Ice, frost, snow and the thawing of these frozen elements during the Arctic summers result in other effects on a periglacial landscape. We've seen how moisture freezing underground can create patterns on the surface of the ground. On a larger scale, this process can create hills and hollows. Snow patches erode hillsides, and frost attacks rocks to form scree slopes or fields of broken rock fragments. The process of thawing can also cause landslips that shape the landscape for many years to come.

Pingo mound

A pingo – an earth-covered ice mound – sits in the tundra landscape of the Northwest Territories, in Canada. A lens-shaped core of ice is expanding underneath the soil and will eventually collapse, creating a crater in the mound.

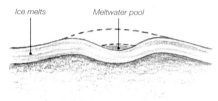

Ice mounds

Where water is trapped on or just under the surface of the ground and is then frozen solid, it forms a large ice core. The ice core gradually expands, causing a mound to form and rise above the ice block.

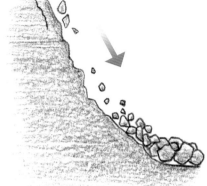

Frost

The cycle of freezing followed by thawing and refreezing is very effective at breaking up rock into large, angular fragments, often resulting in fields of sharp rock debris or scree at the foot of rock slopes (page 74).

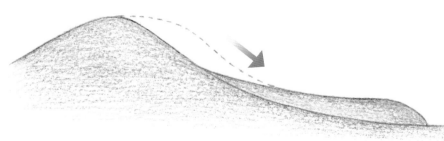

Soil flow

As an upper layer of soil thaws in the summer, it becomes saturated with moisture from thawing ice and snow. Underneath the surface, the lower layers of soil remain frozen and impermeable.

The upper layer is more fluid and slides down the slope over the frozen layer. This process, known as gelifluction, is common in periglacial regions and causes large landslips on slopes and valley sides.

Geothermal Landscapes

Origin of 'geyser'
Strokkur ('the Churn') erupts in a plume of heated water and steam, up to 35m (115ft) high, every ten minutes. It is located at Geysir in Iceland, which gave its name to the phenomenon.

Some parts of the world are still very unstable as a result of tectonic activity, such as Yellowstone in the USA or parts of Iceland. These areas show signs of volcanic activity, where magma rises up to the surface, or earthquakes. Often associated with these areas of tectonic unrest are geothermal features. These are caused by groundwater coming into contact underground with hot magma or rocks heated by rising magma.

Hot rocks

Where cracks in the crust have emerged, at or near the margins of tectonic plates, magma rises through the ground and comes into contact with other rocks, heating them. Rain falls and the water seeps into the ground, working its way down through the layers of rocks. This groundwater reaches the heated rocks or the magma itself. Deep underground, water is heated under greater pressure, meaning that it boils at much higher temperatures than at the surface. The water becomes superheated and rises towards the surface. The closer it gets to the surface, the more the pressure drops and causes the water to be forced up in jets by steam, propelling the water through cracks in the rock to the surface, forming a geyser. As the pressure and water are released, the water jet subsides, and the water falls back to the ground, where it starts to seep underground again. This process is then repeated in a regular cycle. Hot springs are fed heated water slowly and continuously from underground while fumaroles eject clouds of steam and other gases that rise to the surface.

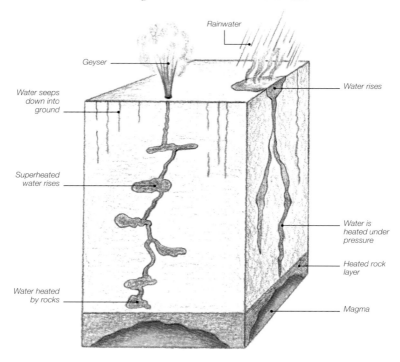

Rainwater

Geyser

Water seeps down into ground

Water rises

Superheated water rises

Water is heated under pressure

Heated rock layer

Water heated by rocks

Magma

Introduction

Throughout this book, we have been considering the natural processes that affect the shape of the landscape and the features that you see within it. And yet, virtually everywhere you look, the landscape has also been affected by the actions of humans. In this section we look at how the land been shaped by human activities, from habitation and agriculture to transport and industry.

Landscape reshaped

So much of what we see today has been affected by humans adapting the landscape to make the most of all available resources. From redirecting rivers, building transport systems, developing agriculture, cutting down trees or planting them, to reclaiming land for development and building seawalls to resist coastal erosion, we have reshaped the land for our convenience.

The human landscape

The landscape has seen many changes since the emergence of human society. Early cultures saw the building of small-scale dwelling structures and farmsteads. In time of war and instability, these were rebuilt to create larger urban areas, often within adapted or specially built fortifications. With political and economic stability, as a result of industrialisation, the need for protection gave way to the need for massive growth in the availability of housing, as well as sites for industrial production and the means for the transport of goods and produce, including ports, canals and roads.

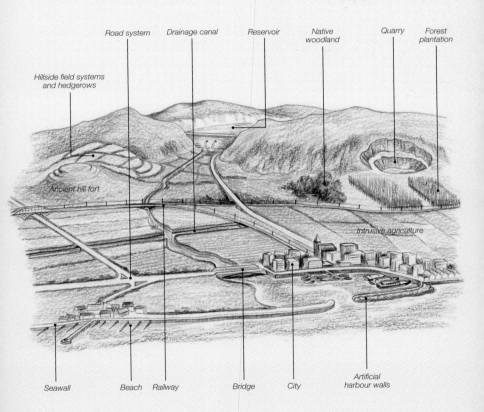

Road system

Drainage canal

Reservoir

Native woodland

Quarry

Forest plantation

Hillside field systems and hedgerows

Ancient hill fort

Intrusive agriculture

Seawall

Beach

Railway

Bridge

City

Artificial harbour walls

Ancient Features

Silbury Hill
Built at the same time as the pyramids in Egypt, around 2400 BCE, Silbury Hill in Wiltshire, UK, is an artificial mound constructed of gravel and chalk. Its purpose is still a mystery.

With the advent of early society, humans looked for places to live, farm and keep livestock, and to protect themselves. At first these societies made use of the available natural features in the landscape, such as caves, hills or islands, but over time, as they grew and became more sophisticated, they adapted the landscape by shaping the ground or building walls and roadways. The landscape still bears the marks of these ancient societies, including mounds and circles built for ceremonial, burial or religious purposes.

Ancient dwellings

Many early dwellings consisted of groups of small roundhouses made from timber, wattle and mud. They left barely traceable circles in the ground. Where wood was less common, stone walls were used.

Fortifications

As larger numbers of people grouped together for security, they often built earth and fence ramparts on natural hills for protection. Ancient cities also used huge walls to protect their citizens.

Agriculture

In many parts of Europe, including the UK, modern field systems still follow the square field patterns ploughed by early medieval farmers. Ploughing on hillsides created banks and terraces or lynchets (above).

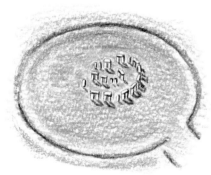

Ceremonial and burial features

Many structures, such as stone circles, including the famous Stonehenge in Wiltshire, UK, were built for ceremonial purposes. Many cultures also built mounds or chambers in which to bury their dead.

Urban Landscapes

Urban areas are rather like natural landscapes in that they have evolved gradually in response to external forces, although over a much shorter period. For at least 12,000 years, humans have gathered to live together for social, economic and political reasons. Early towns and villages grew up near natural resources, such as rivers or natural harbours, or in fortifiable positions for protection. Political stability and the economic growth of an area usually stimulates the expansion of the urban population and the infrastructure to support it.

Tower power

The great sprawling mass of London in the UK, as it is today. The Norman Tower of London, just below and to the right of centre in this photograph, was originally built in the 11th century within the original Roman walls to guard the city. It was then expanded beyond them in the 13th century. Now all traces of the walls have been lost, but the castle's prominent position on the River Thames still remains.

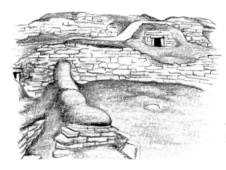

Early habitation

Early dwellings would have been built near natural resources, such as woodland, fresh water or the sea. The landscape may have changed since and there is little chance that their remains can be seen today, but an example can be seen at Skara Brae, Orkney.

Medieval town

As populations grew, and farming methods were able to sustain large numbers of people in close proximity, towns grew up, often with walls for protection. Such towns may have moved or been abandoned if a harbour became silted up, for example.

Industrialisation

With the coming of mechanisation, and increased energy and food supplies, people congregated in towns and cities for work. The landscape was shaped to support transport infrastructure in the form of ports, railway lines and roads.

Natural disasters

All towns and cities change over time, but there may also be sudden changes caused by natural disasters, such as a volcanic eruption (as at Pompeii), earthquakes or floods (as recently in New Orleans) that may substantially change the landscape.

Agriculture

Fresh fields
Hedgerows and fields on mixed farmland in Shropshire, UK. Although the first hedgerows as boundary markers appeared during the Bronze Age, around 1000 BCE, many larger fields were subdivided in England and Wales from the 1300s onwards, and especially between 1720 and 1840 as a result of the Enclosure Acts, when landowners took over and enclosed common land. Intensive farming has begun to sweep away hedgerows like these, which have long been an important habitat for wildlife.

Perhaps the single greatest change to the natural landscape has been made by agriculture. Our ancestors discovered that specific crops could be cultivated to supply food for larger numbers of people. The development of organised agriculture has resulted in the cutting down of large areas of forest – as well as the cultivation of trees for wood as a resource – the importing of soil, the clearing of ground and the draining marshland for farming.

Field systems

The patchwork patterns of fields in rural landscapes are often very old, particularly in Europe, where they may date back to the Bronze Age. Rectangular fields for crops were often created by early plough and furrow techniques. Many crop and livestock field boundaries have since been preserved.

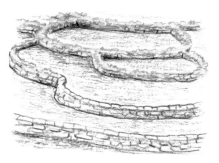

Farm terraces

In hilly areas around the world, and throughout history, farmers have maximised the amount of farmable land by creating terraces of fields for growing crops. The terraces catch water that would otherwise have flowed downhill in order to improve irrigation of crops.

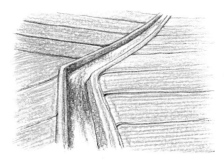

Irrigation and drainage

Many farms rely on regular amounts of water to ensure crops grow as required. In arid areas, this can involve the digging of channels for irrigation. Conversely, channels are also used to carry away excess water from damp and marshy areas, as in the Netherlands, or East Anglia in the UK.

Forestry

Early humans cut down trees in large quantities for wood, and to clear areas for hunting and farming. Some bog or open heathland landscapes result from this ancient clearing work. More recently, trees are planted and harvested on a huge scale for timber and wood.

Reclaimed Land

Palm reading (right)
The Palm Jumeirah resort in Dubai, in the United Arab Emirates. This resort consists of a series of islands that were constructed on land reclaimed from the sea using the latest construction technologies.

As populations grow, the demands for housing or resources increase accordingly. This may lead to the reclamation or creation of land to support further building. The city of Venice in Italy is perhaps the most famous example of humans building on waterlogged land, 'reclaiming' it for habitation, but early Neolithic settlements have been found that used platforms in marshes supported on tree trunks. More recently, land is drained and filled to create suitable sites for large building projects.

Land for building

By the late 1990s, Hong Kong desperately needed to expand its international airport but had run out of land to do so. The solution was to construct an artificial island by levelling two small nearby islands and reclaiming land from the sea. As with many such projects, barriers were sunk into the sea bed and the space between them was filled with aggregate to provide a new platform for the airport's foundations.

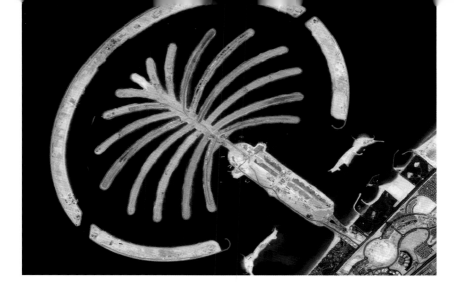

Drainage for agriculture and industry

For hundreds of years, land has often been reclaimed for agriculture from marshland. Much of the Netherlands was drained by great canals, bordered by long artificial dykes or levees. The same engineering, including windmill-powered water pumps, was imported to drain fenland in East Anglia (above) in the UK for agricultural use. In some coastal areas in the past, pits were dug to create artificial saltpans.

Mining & Extraction

As human needs for energy grew from simple wood fires to industrialised burning of fossil fuels, so did the importance of mining. Early mines tended to take the form of open pits or quarries, because the most easily accessible deposits of minerals were the first to be exploited. Today, huge demand for consumer goods has resulted in the need to find greater and greater quantities of natural resources from the ground for processing. Open-pit and underground mining leave long-lasting marks on the landscape.

Open source
Penrhyn slate quarry, Snowdonia in north Wales, UK. Open-pit mining continues today. The seams or layers of the mineral being sought are exposed by the gradual digging and quarrying of the overlying rock. Today, abandoned quarries are often developed for leisure uses, such as visitor attractions – the pits are sometimes flooded to form lakes – and shopping malls.

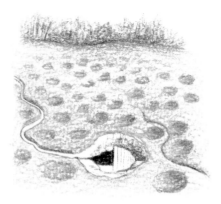

Flint mining

Knapped flint became a sought-after tool for cutting during the Neolithic period. The pits and tunnels at Grimes Graves in Norfolk, UK, are an example of early mines.

Mining for metals

As bronze and iron came into use, so did digging pits to mine for the minerals to make them, including copper (as here at Great Orme in Wales), tin, lead and iron.

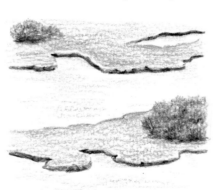

Abandoned pits

Abandoned pits often fill up with water. The Norfolk Broads in England are what remains of medieval peat diggings that have filled with water and vegetation.

Other remnants of mining

Any excavated material, including that from underground mines, has to be brought to the surface, and mounds of discarded material, or spoil, are found near mines.

Coastal Defences

Sea defences
'Hard engineering' techniques have been used for these coastal defences at Hunstanton in Norfolk, UK. A sea wall, concrete steps, and rocks protect the dunes behind, with a wooden groyne to reduce the waves' force and stop the beach being washed away.

We saw on page 160 how erosion attacks coasts and shorelines, changing and reshaping them over time. Where people live, where industry is flourishing, or where there is a demand to protect an area for leisure or wildlife conservation, then resources in the form of several types of artificial structure may be applied to preserve a coastline. Ultimately, in the face of rising sea levels, storms and erosion of the sea bed, such structures can only stave off the inevitable, and a policy of gradual abandonment may be adopted. Today, 'soft' forms of defence are being increasingly employed, such as reintroducing coastal marshland and reedbed to absorb sea intrusions.

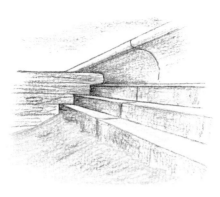

Sea walls

Barriers are often erected at the back of beaches to protect the inland section of a coast. These sea walls tend to be made from reinforced concrete, or from blocks held in wire boxes called gabions.

Large boulders

Another form of barrier often used at the base of sea walls uses large jagged boulders. Called rock armour, the boulders are intended to dissipate and reduce the force of waves as they crash over them.

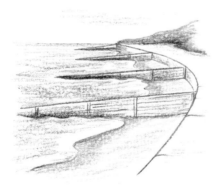

Groynes

A beach protects the coast by reducing the force of the waves. We saw on page 175 how this beach material is carried away by longshore drift. One way of retaining the sand or gravel is to build groynes.

Breakwaters

Another way to reduce the power of the waves reaching the shore is to construct artificial breakwaters. While these protect one area of coast, they can cause changes in currents that affect the coast elsewhere.

Water Features

Humans have adapted many landscape features to control the flow of water for various purposes, such as damming rivers to manage freshwater supplies for the population, to create sources of energy, or to prevent flooding. Humans have also dug canals or redirected rivers in order to provide more efficient transport routes, sometimes on a grand scale. The ground has even been reshaped and artificial ponds, lakes, rivers and waterfalls have been constructed to enhance the landscape. In many cases, particularly after some time, these man-made features can be hard to distinguish from natural landforms.

Hoover Dam
Standing 221m (725ft) high, the Hoover Dam on the border of Arizona and Nevada in the USA was completed in 1936, creating the Lake Mead reservoir behind. It was designed to control flooding of the Colorado River and to generate hydroelectricity.

Reservoirs and artificial lakes

Rivers are often dammed, and valleys then flooded, to create reservoirs that provide freshwater supplies to nearby towns. By damming water, and releasing it slowly, the water can also be used to generate power.

Mill ponds and streams

Water-powered mills began to replace hand grinding as a method of creating flour in 17th-century Europe. Mills were also later used for powering furnaces for iron smelting, for instance.

Canals

Canals were created next to pre-existing rivers in order to provide wider and deeper channels for boats to navigate. Canals have been rendered obsolete by road, rail and air transport – with the exception of large canals such as the Panama and the Suez.

Artificial landscaping

From elegant British Georgian stately homes (such as Stourhead in Wiltshire, UK) to modern golf courses and building complexes, people have shaped the landscape, sometimes on a grand scale, to enhance their living and working environments.

Mapping the Landscape

Maps graphically represent the landscape in a way that anyone can read and follow. So they are a very useful tool for finding your way around as well as predicting the features you are likely to find and helping you to understand how they might have developed. There are several kinds of map, but the most useful in understanding the landscape are topographical maps, familiar to all those who regularly use maps for walking or hiking, and geological maps, which describe the rock formations in an area. This section looks briefly at the history of maps, as well as describing how you can use them to explore and discover a landscape's history.

Reading the ground
Maps can help to tell the story of a landscape as well as help you find your way.

Mapping the Landscape

As humans began to explore the world and plot its resources, so there was a need to record what they found for the benefit of all travellers. With the increasing sophistication of navigation equipment, distances could be measured and recorded more accurately. The same applied to understanding the underlying rock. As a result of the industrial revolution, and the need to find ever more natural resources, the science of geology developed to the extent that maps began to show types of rock in a landscape as well as its topography. Today, the technologies of aerial, radar and satellite imaging, together with GPS (global positioning system), help to plot the Earth's rock structure more precisely.

Mind map

Maps, as much as any other form of literature, communicate ideas. The concept of the Earth as a sphere was well accepted by Greek philosophers by the time of Aristotle (around 350 BCE), although medieval maps, such as the Hereford Mappa Mundi (*c.* 1300), showed how religious views held sway by placing Jerusalem at the centre of the map.

Early maps
Maps have been used for many thousands of years. The earliest known maps were carved onto stone tablets by the Babylonians around 2,300 BCE (above).

Ptolemy's map
By the time of the Romans, mapping had advanced to the point that Ptolemy's world map (*c.* 150 CE and reproduced in 1482) included Africa, Europe and Asia.

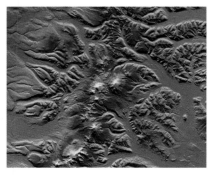

Mercator projection
Maps were printed in large numbers from the 14th century, and Gerardus Mercator invented the cylindrical projection (1569, above), still widely used today.

Modern maps
Modern maps are generated using a range of sophisticated technologies to increase accuracy, such as this radar image of volcanic mountains taken from space.

TYPES OF MAP

Introduction

Today, many types of map are published, including political maps that mark out national and county or state boundaries, for instance, as well as physical maps, which record details of the terrain, such as the contours and shapes of landforms and water depths. Aerial and satellite photography have also helped to generate new forms of map that accurately represent topographical features as well as the underlying rock.

Mapped out
Maps are designed for different purposes. A topographical map like this one is carefully drawn to scale so that measurements can be taken and its user can accurately navigate through the landscape (see page 238). The symbols, lines, colours and notation have also been designed to provide the walker or hiker with useful information.

Political map

A political map outlines the boundaries of cities, counties, states and countries, often using colours to differentiate them. It has probably been one of the most important types of map through the centuries.

Topographical map

Topographical maps show the relief of an area and are particularly useful drawn at a large scale for walkers or hikers. They often show footpaths and landmarks, and use a grid system to help with measuring distances.

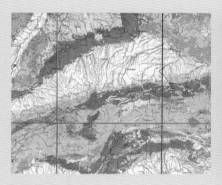

Geological map

A geological map provides a detailed description of the underlying rock structures in a landscape. The geological details are often marked on top of a topographical map with lines, notations and blocks of colour.

Photographic map

Both topographical and geological maps are complemented and often generated these days using photography. Images are taken from an aircraft or satellite, sometimes using special imaging techniques, and then pieced together.

Topographical Maps

The map that is perhaps most familiar to many of us is the topographical or relief map. Primarily used for finding one's way while walking or hiking through a landscape, these maps often include lots of information that can help you to read the geological history of the terrain. For instance, contours and rock outlines, together with river formations, can hint at the origin of a feature and provide a starting point for investigating the geology of a landscape.

Top down

This topographical map provides clues to the form of the landscape. The closer together the contour lines, the steeper the slope. Large white spaces between the lines indicates flatter gradients. With practice, it is possible to read the contours to see if a hillside is convex (steeper at the top than the bottom). Together with a broad, flat valley and a meandering stream, this may indicate that the valley was carved by a glacier.

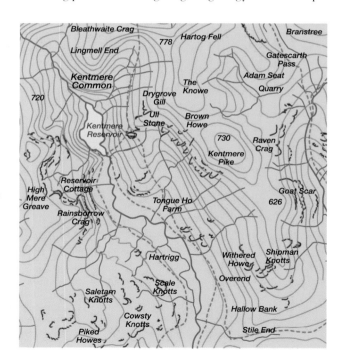

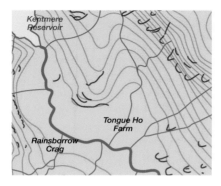

Contours

The contours are marked by the brown lines, with thicker lines indicating height levels. Here they indicate a broad valley bottom with a meandering stream, flanked by steep valley sides carved by glaciation.

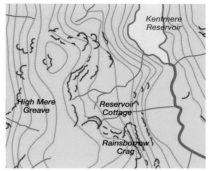

Rock features

Drawn onto the map are also heavy black lines indicating exposed rocky outcrops. The more prominent the rock feature, the more likely it is that it is a hard erosion-resistant rock, probably igneous.

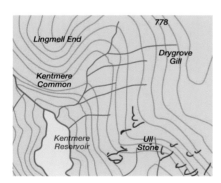

Water

Water on a map can also provide clues to the history of the landscape. Here the sharp indentations in the contours of the valley sides show that water has eroded V-shaped notches down to the valley bottom.

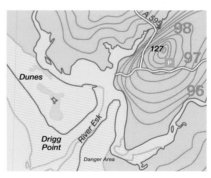

Depositional features

Here a valley widens into an estuary leading to the sea, where mud is being deposited by the river and sand (in pale brown or yellow) is being deposited at the river mouth by shore currents.

Geological Maps

Geological maps are not familiar to the layperson but are used by geologists to understand a landscape's history and the composition of its rocks. These maps contain a huge amount of information. Often overlaid on a topographical map of an area, a geological map describes the position and ages of rock layers and formations. Thanks to Internet web technology, these maps are now readily accessible through the websites of the relevant national bodies (for instance, the British Geological Survey in the UK or the US Geological Survey in the USA).

Digital mapping
Maps like this one are now stored as data sets in a central database, which allows users to build and download their own custom maps over the Internet, sometimes representing the data as three-dimensional models.

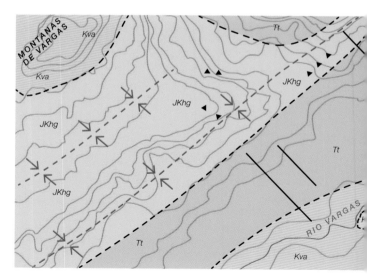

Low down

Geological maps use a number of ways to represent rock formations graphically. The background layer of the map consists of a faint rendering of the topographic map of the area. This helps the user to locate features (and themselves) in the landscape. On top of this layer are placed blocks of colour that represent each type or age of rock layer – also known as a geological unit – and their positions. Abbreviations are used to indicate the age and names of the rock layers. Lines, symbols and numbers represent faults and folds. By analysing a map it is possible for the geologist to begin to draw conclusions about how the layers came to be in these positions.

Key to rock layers

Quarternary rock

QaL *Alluvium*

Tertiary rock

Tt *Tabacón beds*

Cretaceous

Kv *Mafic volcanic rock*

Kva *Valle de Angelis group*

Kk *Krausirpi beds*

Ky *Yojoa group*

Jurassic

JKhg *Honduras group*

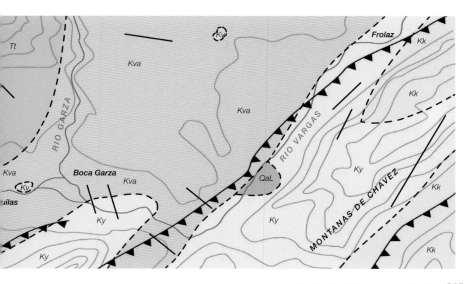

Reading Geological Maps

Lines in the rock
As well as having different thicknesses, lines on a geological map may also be solid, dashed or dotted. These indicate the level of certainty with which geologists can place the boundaries between rock units. For instance, a solid line indicates the known course of a contact line. However, soil, vegetation or building work may obscure a contact from view, so in these cases a dashed line indicates the estimated course of the contact, and a dotted line signifies a much more uncertain course.

At first, the detail in a geological map can seem a little overwhelming. However, once broken down into its component parts, the map begins graphically to tell the story of a landscape. Each block of colour represents a geological unit – or a block of rock of a certain type or age. The lines between the rock describe how the two units came together – by fault or by deposition – and other symbols and notation provide more detailed information. Note that different countries use different standards or forms of map notation, however.

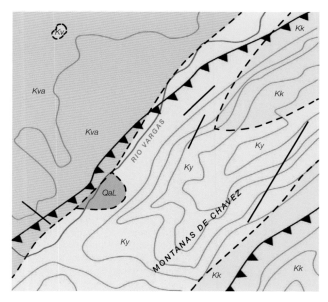

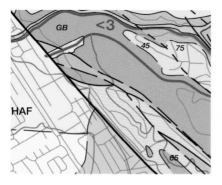

Colour

Each colour indicates a type and age of rock. For instance, an igneous rock may be coloured red and varying ages of sandstone different shades of brown. These colours may differ depending on the map source.

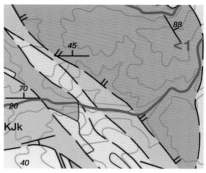

Letters

Each rock type is labelled according to its age. A capital letter represents the period of the rock. For instance, a rock starting with the letter K is from the Cretaceous. Lower-case letters represent the name of a rock.

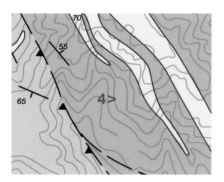

Lines

Where two units of rock meet, this is called a contact, and different types of line define different types of contact. A thin line indicates that one layer was deposited on another, while a thick line indicates a fault.

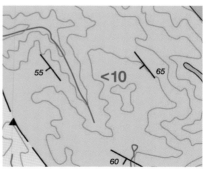

Folds, faults and dip

Folds are shown by lines of medium thickness. Other symbols (e.g. triangles) indicate the type and direction of a fault. Small lines and numbers show the angle and direction (dip) of a tilted rock layer.

Introduction

Mapping things out
You need first to familiarise yourself with the area using a map, and plan your route. Make sure you also know how to use a map, compass and GPS, if you're taking one, before you head off.

Now that you've looked at the map and worked out where you want to go to investigate the landscape further, here is a basic guide to navigating your way, using a map, a compass and a GPS device. Using a map is fairly simple but it is an essential skill, and an important one to learn before you head off, particularly if you're walking in landscapes where the terrain is rough, or where time of day or weather can play an important role in your safety, such as in mountainous regions. Make sure that your clothing, supplies and equipment are appropriate for the terrain and weather.

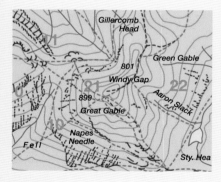

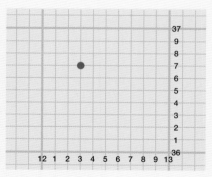

Contours
Understanding how contours work is critical to matching what you see in the landscape to the map, and to finding your way safely. Basically, the closer together the contour lines, the steeper the incline.

Grid system
Using the grid system is also an essential map-reading skill. To find the position of an object, draw an imaginary L to the left and bottom of it, and read off the coordinates along the bottom and then right (123 367).

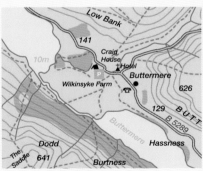

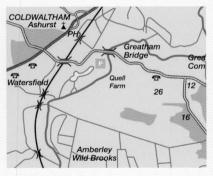

Footpaths and boundaries

Familiarise yourself with all the public footpaths and boundaries along your route before you set out, and make sure that you follow them carefully.

Using landmarks

Preparation is very important, so identify all the landmarks on the map, such as churches, bridges and trig points. Mark them on the map as you pass them.

Using a Compass

Although it is not essential for short walks, a compass is a very useful tool for instantly giving you a fix on the direction in which you are moving. In the dark or in more extreme weather conditions, however, such as heavy rain, fog or mist, when visibility is very poor and you cannot see distant landmarks, a compass becomes an essential tool for finding your way. It is therefore a good idea always to carry one as well as your map.

The right direction
True north and magnetic north are not quite the same as north as shown by your compass. You may have to correct a bearing for magnetic variation. Although this may seem small, you can end up 70m (230ft) off course after a 1km (0.6-mile) walk. Also, carry the correct compass for your region. If you come from the northern hemisphere and are travelling in the southern hemisphere, use the right compass for the trip.

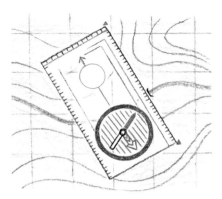

Aligning the map

Hold your map flat and find your current location and your intended destination on it. Now imagine or draw a straight line on the map connecting your position with the point of your destination.

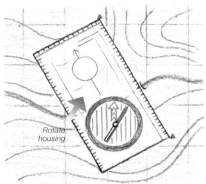

Finding north

Align the long edge of the base plate with this line. Rotate the housing so that the red index line points north at the top of the map. The housing's orienting lines should align with the map's vertical grid lines.

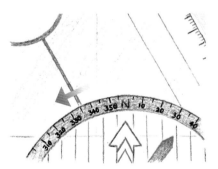

Taking a bearing

Read off the bearing in degrees from the index line on the compass housing. Allow for magnetic variation (MV) – this should be on the key on your map (for instance, around four to five degrees in the UK).

Direction of travel

Walking the bearing

Next, while holding the compass close to you, turn yourself so that the red tip of the compass needle aligns with the N on the housing. Look along the direction of travel for a landmark, and walk towards it.

Using GPS

Getting your fix
In addition to confirming your current location, many handheld GPS units can provide directions to other points entered by the user, as well as a record of the route travelled and distance, time and speed readings. This information can be useful in calculating possible routes. Remember, however, that GPS units need regular recalibration to remain accurate and their batteries also run down, so always be sure to carry a map and compass as well.

The now familiar and popular GPS, or global positioning system, also known as satellite navigation system or SatNav for short, is based upon a network of orbiting satellites originally launched as part of the USA's defence system. A handheld ground-based receiver unit analyses signals from several of these satellites to calculate an accurate positional fix on the ground. There are many types available and now even 'smart' mobile telephones include this facility as well.

Acquiring a signal

Before starting, turn the GPS unit on and make sure it has acquired its position from overhead satellites. While walking, place the unit so that it can constantly receive signals (e.g. in a shoulder-strap pouch).

Using waypoints

A GPS will plot a direct route that you cannot always follow, so it's a good idea to use waypoints. A waypoint is a recorded point, plotted by coordinates. You can enter several from a map to plot your route.

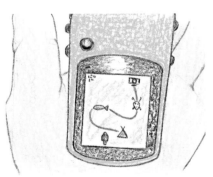

GPS maps

Some GPS units overlay your current location, waypoints and past positions on an on-screen map to help you find your way, but you can also use the unit to check your coordinates on a paper map.

Going home

GPS units can also help you to retrace your steps by directing you back along the route you have followed. Remember to familiarise yourself with the unit before setting off and always carry spare batteries.

Glossary

A'A LAVA Dense, slow-moving, rough-surfaced basaltic lava.

ABLATION The shedding of snow and ice from a glacier by vaporisation and melting.

AEOLIAN Referring to the wind, in particular any landform created by erosion, transportation or deposition by the wind.

AEON The longest division of geological time, spanning several eras. Can also mean a span of a billion years.

ALLUVIUM An accumulation of sediments deposited by running water, including sands, silts, clays or gravels.

ANTHRACITE A hard, highly pure coal with a fixed carbon content in excess of 91 per cent.

ANTICLINE An upward fold in stratified rock.

AQUIFER Rock or sediment that is permeable and porous, letting water flow through it.

ARCHAEAN AEON 3.8 to 2.5 billion years ago, early geological span of time, also refers to age of metamorphosed early Precambrian rocks.

ARCHIPELAGO A group of islands.

ASPHALT Dark cement-like material, composed mainly of hydrocarbons.

ASTHENOSPHERE Part of the Earth's upper mantle below the lithosphere.

ATOLL A ring-shaped island or reef formed of coral that encloses a shallow lagoon and is surrounded by deep water.

BARCHAN A crescent-shaped sand dune that forms where sand supply is limited.

BASALT A dark-coloured, igneous rock, thought to be one of the main components of the oceanic crust.

BASEMENT Metamorphic igneous rock that lies below the oldest sedimentary rocks.

BATHOLITH A huge area of eroded, exposed igneous rock, which originates under the Earth's surface.

BATHYMETRY The measurement of ocean depths and study of the sea floor.

BAUXITE Hydrated aluminium oxide, the principal ore of aluminium.

BEDDING Sedimentary rock, layered with the oldest rock on the bottom and the youngest on the top.

BEDROCK Solid rock beneath the soil or layers of sediment. Bedrock can be exposed at the surface in some locations.

BLOCK LAVA Dense, rough-surfaced lava, also known as a'a lava.

BOG A wetland area rich in vegetation and high in acidity, which slows decomposition and causes peat to accumulate.

BRAIDED STREAM A river or stream that flows in multiple, interweaving channels.

BRECCIA Sedimentary rock, composed of broken or angular fragments.

BUTTE A steep, flat-topped hill.

CALCAREOUS Of limestone, chalky.

CALDERA A large crater formed by a collapsed magma chamber following a volcanic blast.

CAMBRIAN 542 to 488 mya, the first geologic period in the Palaeozoic era.

CAP ROCK A hard layer of rock that protects softer layers beneath from erosion.

CARBON A non-metallic element that is present in all life forms.

CARBONATE ROCK A rock composed primarily of carbonate minerals and oxygen. Limestone rock is the most common example.

CARBONIFEROUS 359 to 299 mya, the fifth geologic period of the Palaeozoic era, when coal- and oil-bearing rock formed from vegetation.

CENOZOIC ERA The most recent and current geological era, covering the period from 65.5 mya to today. The era is framed by the Cretaceous–Tertiary extinction event at the end of the Mesozoic Era and the demise of the last non-avian dinosaurs.

CHALK Soft white limestone rock.

CHERT A sedimentary rock, rich in silica.

CLAST Granulated rock.

CLAY Fine-grained material of sedimentation, sticky when wet.

COAL Metamorphosed carboniferous material, used as fuel.

CONGLOMERATE Coarse-grained sedimentary rock.

CONTINENTAL CRUST Layer of rock lying beneath continents, up to 64km (40 miles) thick

CORE The innermost part of the Earth, comprised of iron and consisting of a solid inner core and a molten outer core.

CRATER A dish-shaped depression created either by a large meteor impact or following a volcanic eruption.

CRETACEOUS PERIOD 145 to 65.5 mya, the youngest geologic period of the Mesozoic era and following the Jurassic period. The end of the Cretaceous period was marked by the significant mass extinction of many species including dinosaurs and large marine reptiles.

CRUST The solid outer layer of the Earth, about 5km (3 miles) deep beneath the oceans and 64km (40 miles) deep beneath mountain ranges.

DEFORMATION Any change in rocks, following geological movements.

DELTA An area of gradually sloping sediment situated at a river mouth.

DENDRITIC A mineral that has many branches, like a fern or tree.

DESERT A dry and usually sandy area with no rainfall.

DEVONIAN PERIOD 410 to 360 mya.

DIP The angle of slope of rock layers.

DOLINE In limestone rock, a steep-sided indentation in the ground that is usually caused by the underground collapse of eroded rock.

DOLOMITE A rock created when limestone changes to calcium magnesium carbonate.

DRAINAGE BASIN A region where water flows towards a single river or lake.

DRIFT Debris transported by glaciers.

DRUMLIN A pear-shaped hill of debris left behind by a retreating glacier.

DUNE A hill of accumulated dry sand by the sea, in a river bed or in the desert.

DYKE In rock, a prominent ridge of igneous rock exposed by erosion of surrounding rock.

EARTHQUAKE The violent movement of the Earth's crust caused by volcanic activity or the movement of a fault.

ELEVATION The height of a point on the Earth, normally measured above sea level.

EOCENE EPOCH 54 to 37 mya.

EON The American spelling of Aeon.

EPICENTRE The point directly above the centre of an earthquake.

EPOCH The subdivision of a geological period.

ERA A division of geological time that covers one or more periods.

EROSION The breakdown and wearing away of soil or rock by wind, water or ice flow and by the debris carried by these agents.

ERRATIC A foreign rock carried by a glacier from its place of origin.

ESKER or **ESKAR** A long ridge of sand or gravel debris, left behind by an ice sheet or glacier.

ESTUARY A stretch of water where a large river meets the sea. The term also applies to inlets and bays where freshwater and seawater combine.

EVAPORITE A sedimentary deposit left by evaporating salty water.

EXFOLIATION The removal of the surface of a rock in layers as a result of weathering.

Glossary

FAULT A fracture in rock causing displacement.

FAULT PLANE The plane or surface along which a fault or fracture has caused movement in the rock.

FISSURE A fracture in the ground or in rocks.

FJARD or **FIARD** A coastal inlet created by the flooding of a low-lying glaciated landscape, without the steep sides characteristic of fjords.

FJORD or **FIORD** A deep, steep-sided sea inlet that has been created by the flooding of a former glacial valley.

FLOOD BASALT An extensive plateau of flat, layered rows of basalt caused by volcanic lava flows and eruptions.

FLOODPLAIN A flat area of land in a river valley, covered with sediment deposited when the river floods.

FOCUS The point at which an earthquake occurs. Hypocentre is an alternative term.

FOLD Rock strata deformed and bent by horizontal compression of the ground.

FOLIATION The arrangement of minerals in leaf-like, parallel layers.

FOSSIL An outline, cast, track or impression of mineralised plant or animal remains.

FUMAROLE A volcanic vent that releases volcanic gases and/or steam.

GABBRO A coarse-grained, dark igneous rock, made from pyroxene, orthoclase and plagioclase.

GEOCHRONOLOGY The science of dating rocks and geological events.

GEODE A circular cavity in rock that often features crystallisation.

GEOLOGY The science of the Earth's history.

GEYSER An opening at the Earth's surface that periodically emits hot water and steam.

GLACIAL REBOUND The rising up of the Earth's crust following the retreat of a continental glacier.

GLACIATION The impact of a moving ice mass on rock.

GLACIER A river of moving ice and snow that slowly moves downhill under its own weight.

GLOBAL POSITIONING SYSTEM A network of satellites that send signals to a receiver unit on the ground, allowing a user to determine their precise location, speed and direction.

GNEISS A banded, coarse-grained metamorphic rock.

GONDWANALAND The ancient southern supercontinent that included Africa, Antarctica, Australia, India, New Zealand and South America. The landmass started to divide 130 mya.

GPS *see* **GLOBAL POSITIONING SYSTEM**

GRANITE A common, granular igneous rock.

GRAVEL A very coarse sediment, mainly comprised of particles larger than 2mm (less than 1/8 in).

GROUNDWATER Water flowing through underground cracks and caverns.

GULLY A small valley with steep sides.

HANGING VALLEY A valley that opens high up a valley side, usually as a result of glaciation.

HEMATITE The mineral form of iron oxide.

HILL A rounded land elevation below 300m (985ft).

HOLOCENE Epoch 10,000 years ago to present.

HUMUS Dark, organic matter found in soil that has formed from dead animals, plants and micro-organisms.

HYDROCARBON An organic chemical compound formed from hydrogen and carbon.

HYDROTHERMAL Of any activity that involves the heating of water by volcanic action.

HYDROSPHERE All the water in the Earth's seas, lakes, rivers and underground spaces.

IGNEOUS ROCK Rock formed from cooled and solidified lava or magma.

INTRUSION The penetration of igneous rock into other rocks while it is in a molten state.

IRON Heavy metallic element, believed to be abundant in the Earth's core.

JOINT A crack or fissure in a rock where there is no displacement, unlike a fault.

JURASSIC PERIOD 206 to 145 mya, the middle period of the Mesozoic era.

KARST An irregular landscape of limestone rock created by extreme erosion, which causes characteristic features, such as pinnacle-like hills or mountains, cave systems, sinkholes and underground streams.

KETTLE LAKE An indentation in the ground caused by melting ice and filled with water.

KOPJE A small, isolated hill rising above a plain.

LACCOLITH A large lens-shaped body of igneous rock.

LANDSLIDE The rapid movement of rock and soil down a mountain or hillside.

LAURASIA The ancient supercontinent, formerly part of Pangaea. The supercontinent included most of the land masses that split around 66 mya to form the continents of the northern hemisphere, including North America, Europe and Northern Asia.

LAVA Hot, liquid molten rock or magma ejected from the surface of a volcano.

LAVA DOME A type of volcano formed by non-gaseous lava.

LAVA FIELD A broad, mostly flat area of lava usually formed by smooth, fluid, basaltic lava.

LEVEE A raised river bank, either natural or artificial, higher than the neighbouring floodplain.

LIMESTONE A sedimentary rock that consists mainly of calcium carbonate.

LIMESTONE PAVEMENT An area of exposed, eroded limestone rock characterised by blocks separated by eroded fissures.

LINEATION An arrangement of any features found in a rock.

LITHIFICATION The process that converts sediment into solid rock.

LITHOSPHERE The outermost solid part of the Earth that includes the crust, plates and continents, and the top part of the mantle.

LOESS An accumulation of sediment deposited by the wind, comprising very fine particles of silt, sand and clay.

LONGSHORE CURRENT A sea current flowing parallel to the shoreline caused by waves approaching the shore at an angle.

LONGSHORE DRIFT The carrying of beach material along the shore by longshore currents.

MAAR A wide, low-lying crater, often filled with water, created by an explosion resulting from groundwater coming into contact with molten magma.

MAFIC A dark-coloured mineral that is rich in iron and magnesium.

MAGMA Hot, liquid, molten rock. Igneous rocks are formed from magma.

MAGNETIC NORTH The point on the Earth where the Earth's magnetic field points 90 degrees downwards.

MANTLE The thick part of the Earth, about 2,300km (1,430 miles) deep, between the crust and the outer core.

MARL A calcium carbonate mud or mudstone, rich in lime.

MASS MOVEMENT Downward movement of surface material caused by the force of gravity.

MEANDER A wide, curving loop in the path of a river.

MESA A flat-topped, steep-sided hill or mountain usually found in arid regions.

MESOZOIC ERA 251 to 65.5 mya, including the Tertiary, Jurassic and Cretaceous periods.

METAMORPHIC ROCK Igneous or sedimentary rock substantially changed by pressure, heat and chemical environment.

Glossary

METAMORPHISM Change in the properties of rock as the result of pressure, heat or the chemical environment.

METEORITE A rock that has fallen from space through the Earth's atmosphere to the ground.

MILLSTONE GRIT A coarse sandstone composed of compressed and cemented small stones and sand grains that were deposited in deltas.

MINERAL Naturally occurring inorganic matter with definite chemical composition and crystalline structure.

MINERALOGY The science of the study of minerals.

MIOCENE EPOCH 23 to 5 mya.

MONADNOCK An isolated hill or mountain left as an erosional remnant on a peneplain.

MONOCLINE An S-shaped fold linking two parts of a horizontal layer at different levels.

MORAINE Deposit of stone or gravel, ground by the movement of a glacier and left at the glacier's side or front.

MOUNTAIN A high hill, usually with steep sides, 300m (985ft) or more in height.

MYA Million years ago.

NAPPE A large area of rock strata folded flat on top of itself.

OBDUCTION The process of a continental plate sinking beneath an oceanic plate.

OBSIDIAN Dark volcanic glass.

OCEANIC CRUST Layer of Earth's crust beneath the oceans, around 5km (3 miles) thick.

OIL Organic hydrocarbon formed from dead and decomposed plant and animal material, found in underground rocks.

OIL SHALE Compressed oil-bearing sediment.

OLIGOCENE EPOCH 34 to 23 mya.

ORDOVICIAN PERIOD 500 to 440 mya.

ORE Metallic deposit or rock mined for refining.

OROGENY The process of mountain building by the compression and upward bending of the Earth's crust.

OUTCROP Exposed bedrock.

OXBOW LAKE A crescent-shaped pool or lake formed by the silting up of a river meander.

PAHOEHOE LAVA Smooth, fluid basaltic lava characterised by a rope-like surface.

PALAEOBOTANY Study of ancient plant life forms.

PALAEOCENE EPOCH 65 to 54 mya.

PALAEOCLIMATE Ancient climate.

PALAEONTOLOGY Study of fossils and ancient animal life forms.

PALAEOZOIC ERA 544 to 245 mya.

PANGAEA The ancient supercontinent from which all continents began to emerge around 200 mya.

PEAT Accumulation of ancient partially decomposed plant material.

PELAGIC ZONE All water to be found in the oceans of the Earth, apart from near the coast or at the bottom of the ocean.

PENEPLAIN A large, mostly flat area of land created by constant erosion.

PERIOD Geological measure of time, subdivision of era.

PERMAFROST Ground that has been frozen for two or more consecutive winters and intervening summers.

PERMIAN PERIOD 286 to 245 mya.

PHANEROZOIC AEON 544 mya to present.

PILLOW LAVA Lava ejected underwater to form pillow-like lumps.

PLATE, TECTONIC *see* **TECTONIC PLATE**

PLATEAU Elevated, flat area of land usually overlying horizontal rock layers.

PLEISTOCENE EPOCH 65 to 54 mya.

PLIOCENE EPOCH 5 to 1.8 mya.

PLUTONIC ROCK Igneous rock that has intruded underground in molten form before cooling below the surface.

POTHOLE Spherical depression in rock made by current-agitated pebble in stream.

PRECAMBRIAN AEON 4,500 to 544 mya.

PROTEROZOIC ERA 2,500 to 544 mya.

PUMICE A very light form of volcanic glass filled with vesicles.

PYROCLASTIC FLOW Mix of rock fragments and hot gases ejected from volcano.

PYROCLASTIC ROCK Rock fragments ejected from a volcano.

QUARTZ Crystals of silicon dioxide. The gemstones agate and amethyst are a form of quartz.

QUATERNARY PERIOD 1.8 mya to present.

REEF Underwater bank or island lying in shallow water, often covered in a build-up of organic material, such as coral.

REGOLITH Layers of earth, soil and loose rock fragments lying on surface of solid bedrock.

RHYOLITE A fine-grained form of igneous rock, similar to granite.

RIA A partially submerged winding river valley that leads to the sea.

RICHTER SCALE Scale used to express magnitude of earthquakes according to the amount of energy released.

RIFT The gap between two blocks of rock caused by faulting.

RIFT VALLEY A valley created by parallel faults causing a central block to slip down.

ROCK A naturally formed mass of solid mineral found in the Earth's crust.

RUN-OFF Water draining across the surface of the ground.

SALINITY A measure of the amount of salt dissolved in water.

SALTATION The movement of sand or fine rock particles in short jumps either in water or above ground when carried short distances and deposited by weak water currents.

SANDSTONE A sedimentary rock consisting of sand grains compacted together.

SCHIST A finely layered metamorphic rock.

SCREE A pile of broken rock fragments at the base of a slope. Also known as talus.

SEDIMENT Fine particles of material deposited by moving water or air.

SEDIMENTARY ROCK Rock formed from the accumulation and compaction of small particle deposits.

SEDIMENTATION Process of forming sedimentary rock.

SEISMIC Related to the shockwaves generated by earthquakes or explosions.

SILL A horizontal ledge of igneous rock formed when molten magma is forced between rock layers.

SILURIAN PERIOD 440 to 410 mya.

SINKHOLE Also known as a doline, a steep-sided depression in limestone caused by the underground collapse of eroded rock.

SLATE Finely layered metamorphic rock formed from compacted shale.

SLUMP A small-scale downward slip of earth or rock.

SOIL Fertile surface material composed of broken and decomposed mineral and organic particles.

SOIL CREEP The slow downhill movement of soil as a result of the force of gravity.

SOLUTION DOLINE In limestone rock, a steep-sided indentation in the ground caused by water dissolving and eroding the rock.

STALACTITE Solidified deposit descending from the roof of a cave.

STALAGMITE Solidified deposit building from the floor of a cave.

Glossary

STRATA Layers or beds of sedimentary rock.

STRATIFICATION Layering of sedimentary rock.

STRIKE The horizontal alignment of a rock feature.

SUBDUCTION The process of one plate sinking beneath another.

SUBSIDENCE Sinking of the Earth's crust below the level of the surface.

SYNCLINE A downward fold in rock layers.

TALUS *see* **SCREE**

TECTONIC PLATE Piece of the Earth's crust that is constantly moving, expanding or shrinking. There are eight major plates and many more minor plates.

TECTONICS The theory that the Earth's crust consists of plates that move on top of the mantle.

TERTIARY PERIOD 65.5 to 1.8 mya.

TIDE The regular rise and fall in sea level as a result of the periodic gravitational pull of the Moon and, less so, the Sun.

TILL Rock debris deposited by a glacier.

TOMBOLO A spit formed of deposits linking an island to another island or the mainland.

TOPOGRAPHY The study of the Earth's surface.

TOR A broken tower of exposed bedrock standing above the ground surface.

TRENCH A deep, long valley in the sea floor.

TRIASSIC PERIOD 245 to 206 mya, the oldest geological period of the Mesozoic era, preceding the Jurassic period.

TUFF Rock formed by the hardening of volcanic ash.

UNCONFORMITY A break in the chronological sequence of rock layers caused by uneven erosion and deposition

UPLIFT The gentle raising of an area of ground by tectonic movement.

U-SHAPED VALLEY A deep, steep-sided valley with a wide floor, usually carved by a glacier.

VEIN A thin deposit of mineral particles in a rock fracture.

VENTIFACT A rock or stone polished by sand or debris blown by the wind, usually in a desert.

VOLCANIC ASH Very fine particles ejected from a volcano.

VOLCANO Typically a conical protrusion above the surface of the ground caused by the ejection of molten lava and ash.

V-SHAPED VALLEY A valley with sides of even slope, eroded by a stream or river.

WADI The Arabic word for a valley in a desert eroded by occasional water flow.

WATERSHED The dividing line between two drainage basins.

WATER TABLE The upper level of groundwater.

WEATHERING The breaking down of rock by the action of heat, pressure, chemicals, rain, wind, frost and ice.

XENOLITH A rock foreign to an area, carried there by igneous activity.

Resources

Bibliography and Resources

BRUNSDEN, D. AND DOORNKAMP, J. (ed.) (1978), *The Unquiet Landscape – World Landforms*, Newton Abbot: David & Charles

BRUNSDEN, D., GARDNER, R., GOUDIE, A. AND JONES, D. (1988), *Landshapes*, Newton Abbot: David & Charles

BUCKLE, C. (1978), *Landforms in Africa – An Introduction to Geomorphology*, London: Longman

CVANCARA, A.M. (1995), *A Field Manual for the Amateur Geologist*, San Francisco: Jossey-Bass/Wiley

FORTEY, R. (2004), *The Earth – An Intimate History*, London: HarperCollins

FORTEY, R. (2010), *The Hidden Landscape: A Journey into the Geological Past*, London: Bodley Head

GILLEN, C. (2003), *Geology and Landscapes of Scotland*, Harpenden: Terra

GOUDIE, A. (1993), *The Landforms of England and Wales*, Oxford: Blackwell

GOUDIE, A. AND GARDNER, R. (1985), *Discovering Landscape in England and Wales*, Hemel Hempstead: George Allen and Unwin

GREGORY, PROFESSOR K.J. (2010), *The Earth's Land Surface: Landforms and Processes in Geomorphology*, Newbury Park CA: Sage

HAWKINS, P. (2008), *Map and Compass – The Art of Navigation*, Milnthorpe: Cicerone

KEAREY, P. (2005), *The Penguin Dictionary of Geology*, London: Penguin

LUHR, J.F. (ed.) (2008), *Illustrated Encyclopedia of the Earth*, London: Dorling Kindersley

LYELL, C. AND SECORD, J. (2005), *Principles of Geology*, London: Penguin

McKIRDY, A., GORDON, J. AND CROFTS, R. (2009), *Land of Mountain and Flood – The Geology and Landforms of Scotland*, Edinburgh: Birlinn

MARSHAK, S. (2007), *Earth: Portrait of a Planet*, London: WW Norton

MITCHELL, C. AND MITCHELL, P. (2007), *Landform and Terrain, The Physical Geography of Landscape*, Eachwick: Brailsford

RENTON, J.J. (1994), *Physical Geology*, St Paul MN: West Publishing Company

THOMAS, M.F. (1994), *Geomorphology in the Tropics – A Study of Weathering and Denudation in Low Latitudes*, Chichester: Wiley

TOGHILL, P. (2000), *The Geology of Britain – An Introduction*, Marlborough: Airlife Press

TURNBULL, R. (2009), *Granite and Grit: A Walker's Guide to the Geology of British Mountains*, London: Frances Lincoln

WAUGH, D. (2009), *Geography – An Integrated Approach* (3rd ed.), Cheltenham: Nelson Thornes

Sources of information on the web

The British Geological Survey's website offers an online service called OpenGeoscience, which includes the geology of Britain, free-to-view geological maps, and GeoScenic, free-to-view photographs for non-commercial uses. www.bgs.ac.uk

The US Geological Survey's website provides extensive topographical, geological and aerial maps of the United States, as well as a range of other geological information www.usgs.gov

For a general round-up of news and useful information about the geology and landforms in the USA and around the world, visit: www.geology.com

Other national geological survey web sites include the following:

Australia: www.ga.gov.au

Canada: gsc.nrcan.gc.ca/index_e.php

France: www.brgm.fr

Germany: www.bgr.bund.de

Iceland: www.os.is

Ireland: www.gsi.ie

Italy: www.isprambiente.it

New Zealand: www.gns.cri.nz/index.html

Norway: www.ngu.no

Spain: www.igme.es/internet/default.asp

Switzerland: www.bafu.admin.ch

Index

Index

Acknowledgements

AUTHOR ACKNOWLEDGEMENTS

I would like to express my profound gratitude to David Robinson for his advice and guidance throughout the writing of this book. I would also like to thank Jason Hook, Lorraine Turner, Michael Whitehead and the team at Ivy for their hard work and support. Finally, I wish to thank my wife Sue for her unstinting love and good humour, and my father for sharing with me his passion for the landscape and geology.